As the host of on[...] vision talk shows, [...] one of the freshest [...] the twenty-something generation. Robert Waldron's book reveals her rise to the top; the setbacks as well as the successes. He examines her career to date including what made director John Waters cast her in the breakthrough role in *Hairspray* and how she went on to lose over 125 pounds to completely revamp her image. He reveals how the cancellation of the series *China Beach* almost ended her rise to fame and then why Ricki Lake went on to become the only talk show host in the US to see her ratings rise in the 1994–95 season.

A *Warner* Book

First published in Great Britain by Warner Books in 1996

Copyright © Robert Waldron 1995

People magazine stories by Peter Castro and Tim Allis
with Jamie Saul were a helpful source of Ricki Lake quotes

The moral right of the author has been asserted.

A CIP catalogue record for this book
is available from the British Library.

ISBN 0 7515 1470 5

Printed and bound in Great Britain by Clays Ltd, St Ives plc

Warner Books
A Division of
Little, Brown and Company (UK)
Brettenham House
Lancaster Place
London WC2E 7EN

"Ricki's Day"

Approximately two hundred eager people are lining up on the street outside the MTI studios in midtown Manhattan, waiting to see their favorite TV talk show host, Ricki Lake. It's a diverse crowd of people, representing several different ethnic backgrounds. Most of them, however, are in their late teens and early twenties. It wasn't that long ago, in the summer of '92, when Ricki could recall staff members scouting the streets, pleading with people to come into the studio so that they could fill out the audience. But that was before *Ricki Lake* premiered and quickly became the number-one favorite among viewers eighteen to thirty-four years old. It's an audience that typically didn't watch daytime talk shows before *Ricki Lake*.

Several hours earlier, at seven-thirty A.M., the alarm rang in Ricki's apartment, rousing Ricki and her husband Rob from their sleep. After taking her dog Dudley for a walk with Rob, Ricki showered, and met with her psychotherapist. At nine-thirty, she visited her gym for an energetic workout. With her body and spirit in sync, Ricki was ready to face the world.

A car picked Ricki up at eleven-fifteen and whisked her to the MTI studio. She was accompanied by Dudley, who Ricki swears resembles actor Dudley Moore. She spent the next half hour doing voice-overs, which included descriptions of upcoming shows and invitations for viewers to be a part of the action if there was a topic that hit close to home. At noon, Ricki met with Executive Producer Gail Steinberg, and several other producers, to discuss the guests scheduled for the upcoming show. Ricki usually tapes six shows in four days, so on some days she tapes back-to-back episodes. The story meeting lasted until one-thirty.

Afterward, Ricki went to her small dressing room, which is filled with candid snapshots of her husband, her parents Barry and Jill, her younger sister Jennifer, and close friends. Dudley followed closely, yapping at her heels. Ricki inspected the various outfits hanging in her dressing room closet and selected what she wanted to wear for the taping. When the show premiered, Ricki was stuck wearing the "talk-show host uniform"—bright-colored clothes that made her look like a perky, first-grade teacher. After discussing it with her producers, however, Ricki got the go-ahead to participate in the decision-making process, and the clothes she sported on the show soon resembled the smart, tastefully tailored clothes she has in her own personal wardrobe.

By two-thirty, the line is snaking around the corner outside the studio, and Ricki is in Hair and Makeup. Nearby is Ricki's trusty phone, which she utilizes during the make-up session to phone friends and family. At the top of the list is an affectionate call to Rob.

Garth Ancier, the other executive producer and co-creator of *Ricki Lake,* is in constant touch with Ricki and staff members from his office in Los Angeles. Monday through Wednesdays, his time is occupied focusing on his other job, as head of programming for the new Warner Brothers TV Network. On Thursdays and Fridays he jets to New York for *Ricki Lake.*

Meanwhile, Ancier's partner and co-creator of *Ricki Lake,* Gail Steinberg, presides over the day-to-day details. At forty-seven years old, the former junior high teacher is the eldest of a forty-person staff whose average age is approximately thirty. With her extensive background in talk shows (beginning with *Donahue* in 1981), Steinberg is considered "the voice of wisdom."

At four-thirty, the energy inside the studio rises several notches as segment producers scurry about, meeting with the guests they've lined up for the show. On days when there are surprise guests added to the mix, who have new information that illuminates what other guests are saying on the show, they're kept hidden away in a different area of the studio. If two shows are being taped, the first one tapes at five o'clock and the second at seven o'clock.

Talking with the guests, the segment producers firmly set the ground rules for the show. It's okay for guests to say whatever's on their minds—in fact, they're encouraged to be vocal—but rising out of their seats to confront another guest is discouraged. They're also directed not to use profanity on the air, or to tell other guests to shut up. Guests are given affidavits to sign, attesting to the accuracy of their stories. If the producers discover that they've provided false details for a chance to appear on *Ricki Lake,* the guests are liable for airfare, ground transportation, hotel bills, and any other expenses accrued by the show during their stay in New York City. Rare, however, is the case of a fraud that slips past Ricki's staff. They work diligently to book guests with honest, sincere stories to share. It's a strict standard set by Steinberg.

As the studio audience is led into the studio, approximately thirty minutes before taping, Supervising Producer Stuart Krasnow greets them with microphone in hand. Besides sharing funny anecdotes with the audience, Krasnow—a former talent coordinator for *Late Night with David Letterman*—works at raising their collective energy by encouraging them to cheer, applaud and stamp their feet.

Several minutes before the taping begins, Ricki is introduced, to an enthusiastic standing ovation. Ricki uses the few brief minutes she has before the taping actually begins to bond with her audience. She reveals tidbits from her personal life, such as her goal to lose fifteen pounds for her starring role in an upcoming movie, *Mrs. Winterbourne*. Ricki also makes fun of her own clumsiness, warning the audience to beware because she could end up in their lap. "I constantly trip and I'm always flubbing, so people see I'm a real person," she says. She shares tales of how her role as a talk-show host has occasionally broadened, such as when she has to discipline a guest.

In an installment titled "Stay Away from My Man," Ricki went on stage and pinched an outspoken guest who wouldn't allow anyone else to speak. "The woman would not listen to me and it was to a point where it was, like, inexcusable," says Ricki. "So I just went on stage, I bent down in front of her and I pinched her on the leg. She shut up and I just said, 'Ma'am, I'm not going to tell you again. You have to be quiet.' " Ricki adds, "I didn't hurt her, but I definitely got her attention." It was also a pivotal moment for Ricki, who learned she had the capability to navigate the show, regardless of how high emotions ran. "That was a big breakthrough for me," she says.

In her stint as talk-show host Ricki has developed an acute knack for identifying people in the audience who bring an electrically charged eagerness to their roles as participants in the fun that's unfolding on the show. "If I see two people in the audience—not that I'm playing favorites or anything—but if I see a young, white guy in the audience, or I see a big, black woman, I'll go to her because she'll have the more outspoken comment nine times out of ten," Ricki says. "It makes the show." Ricki is also quick to compliment or acknowledge audience members who have unique or off-the-wall haircuts. Studio members wearing nose rings also rate a mention.

With mere seconds to spare before the red light blinks on her camera, indicating that the show is in progress, Ricki waits for a cue from her stage manager and turns to the TelePrompTer, which has the text for the show's introduction. For someone who's about to face millions of home viewers across the country, Ricki appears disarmingly relaxed and poised. "I can do this blindfolded now," she says. The two shows run smoothly, without any major surprises—such as the time an irate guest yanked a wig off the woman sitting next to her on stage.

By nine-thirty, Ricki is back at her apartment, where a package is waiting for her. With the package in hand, Ricki greets her husband and plants a passionate kiss on his lips. Once they've caught each other up on their respective days, Ricki sits and opens the package, which contains scripts of the next day's *Ricki Lake.* If the topic is issue-oriented, such as kids bringing guns into the classroom, the package will also contain articles from *The New York Times* or other periodicals that have run articles and stories related to the same subject. Ricki carefully sifts through the information, jotting down points she'd like to address on her show.

After she's finished, Ricki hugs Dudley, and her two cats Annie and Molly, and retires to bed with her husband for a sound night's sleep. She'll need it. "This is the hardest job I've ever had," says Ricki, who's starred in several movies, beginning with her debut performance in *Hairspray,* and who was also a regular on television's *China*

Beach. "It takes so much more focus and commitment than any movie I've ever done. It's like being an actress, except it's more gratifying. Here, my opinion actually means something." She adds, "I still want to be an actress, but I have a brain and I can use it here, and that's nice."

1

"Growing Pains"

The topic of the day on Ricki Lake's phenomenally successful TV talk show was, "I Want to Confront the Pothead in My Family!" Patricia, a middle-aged mom, who hated that her thirteen-year-old son and fifteen-year-old daughter got high, was engaged in a heated debate with her daughter, Jamie. A frustrated Patricia blamed rap music for her wayward children's drug use. Angered by her mom's accusation, fifteen-year-old Jamie bolted out of her chair and began screaming, her arms wildly flailing. Disheartened by the scene, Ricki pointedly interrupted Jamie's tirade and said, "I will not stand here and watch you disrespect your mother!" As Jamie sunk back into her chair, the audience cheered loudly, supporting Ricki's intervention. It was a scene Ricki, in her wildest dreams, could never imagine being played out with her own mom.

In fact, if the producers of Ricki Lake's program suddenly came up with the idea to feature the affable host's family on the show, they'd have to think long and hard to come up with an enticing way to promote the segment—at least compared to the usual topics explored. Unlike the majority of guests who parade across Ricki's cozy set, complaining of slights they've suffered at the hands of their parents, siblings, spouses and significant others, Ricki has pointed out that she's perfectly happy with her own family. To lure viewers to the program, the producers would probably have to tout such sensational, attention-grabbing subject titles as:

"My Parents Are So Supportive It Scares Me!"

"My Sister and I Are So Close We're Practically Siamese Twins!"

"I Feel like an Outcast because I Come from a Well-Adjusted Family!"

Ricki, who was born on September 21, 1968, grew up in Hastings-on-Hudson, New York. In interviews, Ricki describes Hastings as "a perfect American town, just north of New York City." Ricki's dad, Barry, operated his own pharmacy, while her mom, Jill, took care of the household responsibilities. A year after Ricki was born, her parents were blessed with a second daughter, Jennifer. "When we were growing up, my sister and I looked alike, but we were complete opposites. I was the outgoing one; she was the quieter one," said Ricki.

Ricki's natural-born gift for performing surfaced at an early age. She identified herself as a *Sesame Street* baby. The long-running program premiered when Ricki was a year old, making her a first-generation follower of the ground-breaking series. When she was five years old she shocked her mom by sitting down at the piano and playing from the sheet music in front of her. Whenever possible, Ricki also entertained her family by grabbing a candlestick, planting her feet in the middle of the living room and belting out songs. "From the time I was very little, I always wanted to please others by putting on a show," she said.

Anxious to take her talents beyond playing piano and singing songs for her close circle of family and friends, Ricki made a stunning announcement when she was five years old. Inspired by the programs she saw on television, which featured young children, Ricki revealed that she wanted to be an actress. "I wanted to be a TV star from when I was little," she's said. Her secret wish was that the actress who played the youngest tot, Cindy, on *The Brady Bunch* reruns she watched religiously

would get sick and that she'd be called upon by the
producers to take over the role. Unhappy with her
name, Ricki even gave herself a new, more feminine one that she hoped would propel her to star-
dom: Laura Ingalls (based on a popular character
from another TV series she enjoyed watching, *Little House on the Prairie*). "Ricki is my real name, I
swear!" she told a *USA Today* reporter. "And to
this day, I hate it," she added. "I wanted something more feminine, like Erica."

Moving her daughter's performing skills out of
the family living room and into a larger arena, Jill
enrolled Ricki in ballet lessons. Looking back on
her years of studying formal ballet, Ricki said, "I
loved it. I was the center of attention." Nevertheless, as much as she enjoyed the dance lessons, and
the lavish attention she netted from wearing a
tutu and performing precise pirouettes, singing remained her first love. This became abundantly
clear to Jill after she took Ricki to see her first
Broadway musical, *Annie*, when she was eight
years old. The show, which told the poignant tale
of a young orphan girl, introduced Ricki to a world
where youngsters who were her peers performed
before thousands of people who actually paid to
watch them. "It made me realize that kids my age
could sing and act in front of people," she recounted. Ricki enjoyed the experience so much

that she didn't want to see the musical end. As the houselights went up, Jill found her daughter weeping because she wished *Annie* could've lasted longer.

When they returned home, an enthusiastic Ricki breathlessly shared with her grandmother the magic she had witnessed on the expansive Broadway stage. By the time she was nine years old, Ricki had memorized the entire score of *Annie*. Ricki's grandmother urged Jill to enroll Ricki in singing lessons, but for a long time Jill resisted it. Although ballet lessons were practical because they helped to develop poise, Jill had her doubts about how much Ricki would benefit from singing lessons in the long run. She was also reluctant to encourage Ricki's goal to become a professional singer and dancer, just like the kids she had seen in *Annie*. "I wasn't fat then—just a little plump," said Ricki, "but one reason my mother didn't want me to take singing lessons was that she didn't want me to experience rejection. I didn't have the typical child-star 'look'—blond, blue-eyed and thin—and in my mother's eyes, that meant I wasn't 'commercial' enough." However, when a persistent Ricki continued to plead with her mother for voice lessons, Jill finally relented. Grateful for the lessons, Ricki soaked up everything she could learn, and continued taking them for the next nine years.

At age thirteen, Ricki took a huge step in making her dream to become a professional performer a reality. She scoured *Backstage* and *Show Business* for ads requesting the talents of people in her age range. When Jill declined to accompany Ricki to New York City for the open auditions, a determined Ricki made the forty-minute train ride on her own. After each audition, Ricki would scurry home, hoping she'd receive a phone call announcing she had won the part. Eventually, Ricki succeeded in landing featured singing roles in two off-Broadway reviews, *The Early Show* and *Youngstars*. Feeling vindicated in winning the parts, Ricki used them as examples to show her mother that she could forge a successful career in show business. But to Ricki's frustration, Jill remained unconvinced. Although her heart would swell watching Ricki perform, Jill still feared that Ricki's unwavering desire to pursue a professional acting and singing career would only lead to unending rejection and ultimately destroy her spirit.

Whenever possible, Ricki also attended Broadway musicals. To savor the experience more, Ricki saved the Playbill from every show she ever attended, including her first, *Annie*. In her room at night, she'd pore over the Playbills, reading the actors' biographies, searching for clues on how they got their first big break. Eventually, she collected over 150 Playbills, including vintage ones that her mom had purchased for her from such bygone musicals as *Annie Get Your Gun*.

When Ricki was fifteen years old she persuaded her parents to let her transfer from her local high school to the Professional Children's School, a private school in New York City for youngsters who performed professionally. Ricki loved attending the school because it enabled her to interact with other children who shared her dream of becoming a star. Judging from at least two of the students who attended the Professional Children's School at the same time as Ricki, she had more than ample opportunity to rub shoulders with other adolescents who were also serious about honing their craft. Her classmates included Christian Slater and Martha Plimpton, who eventually enjoyed starring roles in several big-budget motion pictures. It was a far cry from her local school, where her former classmates had other things on their minds besides show business. Looking back on that period of her life, Ricki told *TV Guide*, "I did not want to sit around and get drunk like a lot of high school students did. I really wanted to be perfecting my craft." While enrolled at the Professional Children's School, Ricki appeared at such New York-area cabarets as Don't Tell Mama, landed a few roles in commercials and secured bit parts on various television series, including *Fame* and *Kate and Allie*. In an interview with the *Village Voice,* Ricki kiddingly revealed that she terrorized Ari Meyers, a young actress who had a costarring role on *Kate and Allie* as Susan St. James's daughter.

Although Ricki was plump in high school, it didn't hold her back from dating or participating in sports, at least during her early high school years. "I was one of the most athletic kids in school," she said. "I was in every activity. I always had boyfriends—always, always. It's an attitude. If you're happy with yourself, then others are too." With her winning personality and outgoing nature, Ricki was also considered one of the most popular and admired students in her class. "In high school I doted on the fact that I had not one enemy. I only wanted for people to be able to say nice things about me, so I did a lot for my friends. I still do," she said.

But as Ricki approached her senior year, she noticed a dramatic weight gain. When she stopped to weigh herself on the scale in her family's bathroom, Ricki realized she could no longer describe herself as plump. With her weight creeping toward two hundred pounds, Ricki recognized that she had become overweight. "I was eating a lot of junk food and I never exercised—I had even stopped going to gym class," she revealed. "This combination made my weight balloon."

At the same time Ricki was attending the Professional Children's School, she enrolled in her first adult acting class. But her stint with the class, where she was one of the youngest members, was short-lived. A headstrong Ricki ignored the instructor's advice and tried to do things her own way. Eventually, she was dropped from the class. "My teacher said I wasn't mature enough or serious enough about my acting," explained Ricki.

Unfortunately, Ricki's various setbacks during her later high school years only served as fuel for her mom to continue discouraging her show-biz aspirations. "A lot of what Ricki has is due to her own tenacity," observed her sister Jennifer. "Mom was always making excuses, saying, 'Wait until your braces come off,' or, 'Wait till you lose some weight.' I think my parents were trying to protect her because they felt she wasn't the typical ingenue." In a desperate attempt to try to influence Ricki to envision other career options, Jill even suggested she consider going into plumbing.

After graduating from the Professional Children's School, Ricki bowed to her parents' wishes that she postpone her show-business plans until she first attended college. But after submitting several college applications, Ricki found that only one school would accept her, Ithaca College in Ithaca, New York. Biting the bullet, Ricki filled out the necessary papers and enrolled at Ithaca.

After a few short weeks at the school, however, Ricki found herself feeling completely miserable and disheartened. She didn't even find solace in Ithaca's drama department. "The theater group there didn't cast me *once* in any of the plays," she said. Adding insult to injury, most of the classes in the drama department were scheduled early in the morning. "I had my voice and movement class at eight o'clock in the morning," recalled Ricki. "I can't open my eyes at eight in the morning, let alone grunt like a pig."

In a futile bid to drop out of Ithaca, Ricki applied for a part-time job, hoping that she'd be able to demonstrate to her parents that she could earn money while auditioning for acting roles. Alas, Ricki's job search didn't net her one offer, not even from The Gap. "When you don't get a callback from The Gap, you know you're in trouble," Ricki conceded. "I knew I wasn't overqualified; the only job I ever had was babysitting."

Unable to envision herself spending another three years at Ithaca, Ricki gathered her parents in their living room for a serious heart-to-heart. "I made this deal with my parents," she said. "I really hated going to Ithaca College, so after finishing my freshman finals, I decided that I wanted to give a try at show biz for a solid six months. The deal was that if nothing turned up in that time, I'd go back to school."

As her freshman year was drawing to a close, Ricki's weight had passed the two-hundred-pound mark. Although Ricki didn't see her weight as a hindrance, her parents certainly didn't view it as an asset. Tired of quarreling with their daughter about her career plans, an exhausted Barry and Jill agreed to the deal a reasonable Ricki had pitched. As far as they were concerned, it was a win-win situation for them. If Ricki was unable to land steady acting work, she'd be back in college by the following year. Meanwhile, on the off chance that she was able to land her big break, they'd be able to take comfort in knowing that their daughter had become a success in a field where failure was more often the norm.

But before Ricki even officially dropped out of Ithaca College, she received a call from her agent saying that director John Waters was casting a new movie and that there was a part in it that was perfect for her.

It later proved to be a call that would change Ricki's life forever.

2

"Hairspray"

When Ricki received the call from her agent about a starring role in a new film, tentatively titled *Hairspray*, she had reservations about making the five-hour drive to New York to audition. Although her agent said the part called for an overweight young woman, Ricki suspected the money wouldn't be very good because it was a low-budget film. "But it's a *John Waters* movie!" her agent implored.

"Yeah, who's that?" asked Ricki.

Ricki's lack of knowledge about director John Waters was understandable. At nineteen, she wasn't familiar with a string of low-budget movies John Waters had filmed in the sixties and seventies in Baltimore. His first feature, *Mondo Trash,* was completed in 1969 on a budget of twenty-one hundred dollars. Production on the film ceased

when the director and two actors were arrested for
"participating in a misdemeanor, to wit: indecent
exposure." Starring in the movie was a boyhood
friend of Waters, Glenn Milstead, also known as
Divine, a character actor who was successfully
able to play both male and female roles. Waters
and Divine worked on several other movies together, including *Multiple Maniacs,* an intriguing
story of circus freak-show hosts who terrorize unsuspecting suburbanites; *Pink Flamingos,* which
featured two families fiercely competing for the
title of "The Filthiest People Alive" (in one scene
Divine stoops down and eats dog excrement off a
curb); *Female Trouble,* in which Divine appeared
in dual roles, as a demented juvenile delinquent,
Dawn Davenport, and as Dawn's welder-lover,
Earle Peterson; and *Polyester,* the first film to be
made in Odorama, with scratch-and-sniff cards
pegged to specific scenes. Critics were sharply divided on Waters's work, much of which had
reached the status of cult classic (*Pink Flamingos*
ran in Los Angeles and New York for eight consec-
utive years). *The Village Voice* hailed Waters as a
"true original," while Rex Reed dismissed his
films as "trash." Meanwhile, Waters's hometown
newspaper, *The Baltimore Sun,* affectionately
dubbed him "The Prince of Puke." Describing his
films Waters said, "I like anxiety-provoking

humor. I'm interested in how something that's so horrible in real life can be laughed at on the screen."

After getting a quick rundown over the phone of Waters's screen credits, Ricki was still reluctant to show up for the audition because she knew that the offbeat filmmaker hadn't asked to see her specifically. Instead, it was an open cattle call, meaning that Ricki would compete for Waters's attention against dozens of other overweight young women.

What Ricki didn't know was that Waters was knee-deep in an extensive search to find an unknown, albeit overweight, young actress to star in his latest movie. "We looked all over the country and read lots of people," said Waters. Finally, he had narrowed the search down to New York City. "I had a casting agent in New York," he said. "I saw a lot of fat girls. It was great. Some of them would come in and I'd say you're not fat enough." Recalling one memorable young woman, who broke down and wept after hearing she wasn't heavy enough for the part, Waters said the struggling actress told him "she'd spent two years losing weight because she was always too *fat* for parts."

Realizing this was a rare opportunity, and one that Ricki shouldn't pass up, her agent, who was growing more and more frustrated hearing her apprehensive young client's multitude of reasons for not making the audition, finally cut to the chase and managed to put everything into perspective by saying, "There aren't that many roles that you're right for. Just go ahead and read for them."

Although Ricki was in the middle of finals at Ithaca College, she hopped into her car in the middle of the night and headed for New York City. Before she reached her destination, however, Ricki's car broke down. Stranded on a highway, Ricki debated throwing in the towel and heading back home. But the conversation she'd had with her parents a few days earlier about making a firm commitment to search for acting roles during the next six months loomed large in her mind. Taking a deep breath, Ricki reached into her purse and collected enough change to phone for help so she could get her car operating again. With the help of the Triple A, Ricki was soon back on track and heading for New York City.

When she arrived at the audition's reception area, where several young women had gathered, nervously anticipating the moment when they'd have their chance to meet with the director, Ricki's heart quickly sunk. Granted, the young women were overweight, but many of them were also strikingly attractive. "I knew I wouldn't get the part," said Ricki. She felt like she had wasted her time traveling all the way to New York City on the off chance that she would win the starring role in what was after all just a low-budget movie. After registering with the receptionist at the desk, Ricki took a seat next to a young woman she vaguely recognized. "She had one of those beautiful faces," recalled Ricki, who quickly sized her up as a "fat people's model." In an effort to get her mind off the audition and her gnawing insecurities, Ricki watched as the girl primped herself. With a genuine tone of sincerity, Ricki made eye contact with the young woman and said, "You're really pretty." Flattered by the compliment, the young woman smiled broadly and responded, *"Fank you!"*

Remembering the moment, Ricki explained, "She had a major speech impediment!" Sitting back in her chair, Ricki grinned to herself and realized that maybe she did have a shot at landing the role. Her confidence soared when she watched the young woman leave the reception area thirty seconds after she had walked into the adjoining office to meet with John Waters.

Soon after, Ricki was escorted in and introduced to Waters. "I'm not what you call introverted," admitted Ricki, a fact which quickly became clear to Waters. Upon Ricki's introduction to him, she immediately noticed that the whites of both of his eyes were red. Before Waters had the chance to say, "Nice to meet you," Ricki blurted out, "Eeeoooh! What's *wrong* with your eyes?"

Rather than feeling self-conscious or offended, Waters smiled and quietly responded, "Oh, I've had this all of my life."

Feeling her face go flush, Ricki suddenly put her hand to her mouth and said, "Ooops! That was so rude of me. I'm so stupid and I'm sorry!"

Ricki's candor, however, was a breath of fresh air for Waters, compared to the hundreds of girls who had been unceasingly polite. In fact, Ricki's direct, but sweet, nature reminded Waters of Tracy Turnblad, the lead teenage character in *Hairspray*. Excited by his find, Waters put Ricki at ease by protesting, "No! That's perfect! That's *exactly* what Tracy would have said."

At the audition, Ricki dressed in extremely baggy clothes. Initially, it prompted Waters to silently speculate about the hopeful young actress's actual size. "John kept looking over his desk to see if I was really big or trying to make myself look bigger," said Ricki.

Nevertheless, Ricki impressed Waters enough to be called back for a screen test. Reading the screenplay of *Hairspray* in preparation for the test, Ricki felt elated. Set in Baltimore during 1962, *Hairspray* was a music-filled comedy revolving around a popular local *American Bandstand*-type TV dance program, *The Corny Collins Show*. The teenage stars of the show are Amber Von Tussle, whose nouveau-riche parents live in East Baltimore, and the handsome Link Larkin, an Elvis-lookalike. The show's biggest fans are Tracy Turnblad and her best friend, Penny Pingleton, who rush home from school every afternoon and plop themselves in front of the tube to catch the latest dances. Tracy's goal is to become a regular on the dance show. But there's just one obstacle standing in her way. She's overweight. Through sheer determination and self-will, a passionate Tracy manages to win a spot on *The Corny Collins Show,* and even becomes romantically involved with Link, much to Amber's chagrin. Meanwhile, Tracy's friend Penny falls for a black student, Seaweed, who'd also like a chance to dance on *The Corny Collins Show*. Unfortunately, because of the times, the show is segregated. Angered by the unjust "whites only" policy, Tracy jeopardizes her own standing on the show to try to integrate it.

Describing the movie, Waters said, "It's a period I remember very well; both a terrible time and wonderful time, when everyone looked absolutely insane and it wasn't a rebel look, it was the norm. 1962 was right before everything changed." Further reflecting on the seemingly innocent period of the early sixties, Waters added, "Kennedy wasn't shot, the Beatles hadn't started, there were no drugs, and that teased-hair look was kind of the norm. A lot of people's mothers had that look—beehives—which is still to me a lot more bizarre than a Mohawk."

After reading the screenplay, Ricki felt excited about the prospect of playing Tracy. Not only was it a glamorous leading role, but she'd have the chance to play a heroine who also fell in love and ended up with the romantic male lead. "Tracy's not inhibited in the least," Ricki noted, "and that's the way I've always been. I've never been taunted or teased, I've always had my share of friends and that's exactly what she's like. She's respected for who she is and not what she looks like."

To prepare for the screen test, Ricki asked her mom, who had been a teenager during the early sixties, to teach her several popular dances from the period, including the Mashed Potato. After hauling out her mom's dusty record collection from her bygone teenage years, Ricki practiced relentlessly over the next few days. Although she was able to skillfully master several of the steps, Jill took exception to Ricki's interpretation of the Mashed Potato, and later said, "I still don't think she does it right."

When Ricki arrived for her screen test, Waters immediately set out to make her feel comfortable. "John was terrific," offered Ricki. "He introduced me to everyone there." At the test, Ricki was asked to dance. Thanks to the crash course lessons provided by her mom, Ricki dazzled everyone on the set, including Waters. Soon after, Ricki learned she'd landed the part.

"I needed someone who was big and pretty and could act and dance," said Waters. "Ricki had a great laugh and basically said, 'I'm Tracy, I can be that, I've always been that type of girl. I've always been big, I'm not uptight about it and I've always been a leader.'"

Once Ricki had the role, she was informed that Divine would be playing her mom, Edna. Although Ricki hadn't the slightest idea who Divine was, she smiled broadly and said, "Great!" When Ricki arrived home, however, and informed her mom of the news, she was in for a revelation. "She died laughing," Ricki recounted, "told me that Divine was a man, and then said I looked more like Divine than her!"

At first, the news about Divine's actual identity troubled Ricki. "I was really worried that, because I play Divine's daughter, people would think I was a man, especially because my name is Ricki," she explained. But after giving the matter further thought, Ricki let her insecurities about being mistaken for a guy fall by the wayside and focused on preparing for her first feature-film role.

Before pre-production had started on *Hairspray,* when it was still a screenplay that Waters was shopping around to various Hollywood studios, Divine had hoped to snare the role of Tracy, as well as the part she was eventually cast to play as Tracy's mom, Edna. "I wanted to do it, to play both mother and daughter, like those Lana Turner movies where she was sixteen years old and then she's eighty," Divine told *Interview* magazine. "I thought it would add the right touch. But I think the producers were a bit leery, so they hired Ricki Lake to be my daughter."

Actually, Waters had also originally envisioned Divine playing Tracy, and wrote the part with Divine in mind. But ultimately, Waters, who was trying to broaden his audience beyond the loyal cult fans who attended midnight screenings of his earlier films, realized he would have difficulty finding investors to back a movie which featured a middle-aged male character actor dressed as a teenage girl, especially if the girl had romantic scenes with an actual teenage boy. So he sat down and revised his script, beefing up the role of Edna, with Divine pegged for that part. But even with that casting concession, Waters experienced difficulty trying to

sell the movie to various Hollywood studios. By the
time Waters met with New Line Cinema, which
eventually produced the film, he had already
pitched *Hairspray* to three other Hollywood studios. The first two immediately dismissed it. But
the third studio expressed interest. "It got ap-
proved at two levels at one studio—I won't say
which one—" recounted Waters, "before the main
guy said no." Apparently, the high-ranking executive grew squeamish and turned *Hairspray* down
after viewing *Pink Flamingos*. "It always hap-
pens," noted Waters. "They watch my old work at
ten A.M. in their offices and have a nervous break-
down." As a joke, Waters added, "*Pink Flamingos*
is the film that gets me *in* the door and then
thrown *out* the door."

Even New Line Cinema was initially opposed to
casting Divine in *Hairspray,* regardless of what
role he played, because executives fretted that Waters and Divine working on a film together again
would prompt comparisons with their earlier movies. In the end, however, Divine was cast as Edna.
Milstead also landed a second, smaller role in the
film as Arvin Hodgepile, the racist station manager who only allowed blacks to dance on *The
Corny Collins Show* on "Negro Day."

Once Ricki was cast as Tracy she had two days
to prepare before flying off to Baltimore, where the

movie would be filmed on location. Meanwhile, Ricki never completed her freshman finals at Ithaca College, choosing instead to drop out so that she could make the first day of filming for *Hairspray*. Nor did she ever look back with regret.

"Nothing in my life since *Hairspray* has just *happened*," said Ricki. "It's fate."

3

"Summer Camp"

As Ricki prepared for her first starring role in a feature film, she didn't realize the magnitude of what was happening to her. *Hairspray* was scheduled to shoot over the summer of 1987, which meant while Ricki's acting friends, who were still hoping for their big break, would be spending the next few months waiting tables or folding jeans at The Gap, Ricki would be involved in a fun-spirited adventure, meeting new people and having the chance to flex her acting muscles. Nor did she allow herself to think the movie would lead to more roles. After all, if she had never heard of John Waters or Divine, what were the chances that her peers, who made up a significant percentage of the movie-going audience, knew of their work? As far as Ricki was concerned, she viewed her break as "a summer job to make a couple of bucks."

Before the cameras started rolling, Ricki was hit with what she felt was horrifying news. Waters wanted to dye her light-brown hair a darker shade and tease it. "I didn't want to dye my hair," recalled Ricki, who was also disheartened by the idea of having an unknown stylist take a pair of scissors to her head to trim her tresses. "It had taken me three years to get it all one length," said Ricki, in defense of her resistance to follow Waters's directive. For the next few days, several conversations ensued between the hesitant leading lady and troubled director over the telephone as she tried to change his mind. "Couldn't I just wear a wig?" she tearfully pleaded at one point. In the end, Ricki finally caved in to Waters's directive. Her hair was dyed and teased. The experience taught her a valuable lesson. On a movie set directors have the final word, even when it comes down to your appearance—at least if you're a novice actor just starting out. Maintaining a philosophical attitude about it, a good-natured Ricki even came to understand Waters's position. Echoing what she assumed was Waters's viewpoint, she told *TV Guide,* " 'The bitch better well dye her hair to keep the lead role in *my* movie.' "

*   *   *

In mid-June, Ricki packed eight bags of luggage, picked up a coach-class ticket and headed for Penn Station, where she was scheduled to board a train from New York City to Baltimore, Waters's hometown. After bidding her parents and sister Jennifer a tearful farewell, an apprehensive Ricki set out to find Michael St. Gerard, the young actor who'd be costarring with her in *Hairspray* as well as playing her love interest and who would be waiting for her at the station. The studio had described St. Gerard as dark and handsome, with smoldering looks that resembled Elvis Presley (a comment St. Gerard often heard, and one which would pay off in spades when he was cast a few years later to play a young Elvis in a short-lived series about the legendary singer's life that aired on ABC-TV in early 1990). Spotting St. Gerard, Ricki felt her heart stop. The studio executive who'd described St. Gerard was dead on the money. Ricki thought he was drop-dead gorgeous. After catching her breath, she suddenly thought to herself, "God, how did they describe me to him, a combination of Miss Piggy and Bette Midler?" With a warm, friendly smile, St. Gerard introduced himself to Lake and they boarded the train.

During the train ride, Ricki and St. Gerard had ample time to get acquainted. They swapped amusing stories about their childhoods and their passion for acting. Although Ricki was initially nervous meeting St. Gerard, she quickly grew comfortable. St. Gerard, meanwhile, understood why Waters had selected Ricki to play Tracy. She was funny, personable and very easy to like. By the time the train inched its way into Baltimore, Ricki and St. Gerard had become good friends. Soon after, St. Gerard confessed to Ricki, "I thought you would be much bigger." His kind, well-intentioned words meant more to Ricki than St. Gerard realized. "I loved him for that," she said.

Waters's reason for shooting *Hairspray* in Baltimore, just as he had his first ten movies, was largely practical. "It's easier to do things here. If we need six sets of false eyelashes at two A.M., we know where to get them," he explained. With ten other films under his belt, Waters had also built up a crew of loyal and talented people. For each movie he relied heavily on casting director Pat Moran, who was also his best friend. With *Hairspray*, Moran would definitely earn his salary. During the summer shoot he was responsible for casting more than a thousand extras. Waters also employed the services of his longtime friend, Vincent Peranio, who worked as his art decorator. Since *Hairspray* was set in the early sixties, Peranio had his work cut out for him. But he found the experience easy-going because of the work relationship he shared with Waters. "We work together almost instinctively," said Peranio. For example, when Peranio was called upon to design a space-age car, he revealed, "All John said was, 'Make it futuristic and make it stupid.'"

During the shooting of *Hairspray*, the city of Baltimore would play a significant role in the movie. With a smile, Waters describes his hometown as "the hairdo capital of the world. I've always liked to watch hair." Recalling *The Buddy Deane Show,* a local American Bandstand-type show that inspired Waters to write *Hairspray,* he says, "The most popular girl on the show was Mary Lou, who had really high hair that she wore in a 'double bubble' one day, an airlift the next. She disappeared one day from the show, and rumor had it that roaches had infested her hair." Waters was so taken with the legendary rumor that he used it in *Hairspray,* when a rival leveled the same charge against Tracy.

Looking back nostalgically on the period, when teased styles were the rage, Waters added, "When the straight-hair fashion first hit our neighborhood it caused a panic. Your whole life values changed. If you had ironed hair, you became a hippie. And if you kept your hair teased, you got mar-

ried at twenty and had four kids. Hair was politics.
Now, if you're a skinhead, you could be a punk or
a Nazi. Who knows? My mother says to me now,
'Thank the Lord you're not sixteen today. You'd
have a Mohawk!' "

Waters exercised great care in recapturing the
Baltimore of his teenage memories. To lend authenticity to the movie, he bypassed the traditional route of using familiar Motown tunes and
instead selected rare, vintage songs that lent a
unique flavor to the movie's musical score. Songs
selected for *Hairspray* included the rarely heard
Touissant McCall's "No One Takes the Place of
You" and Lesley Gore's "You Don't Own Me."
With more than a thousand performers to style
and make up for the summer shoot, a total of sixty
cases of hair spray were used to re-create the
teased-hair look. Waters also employed a former
dancer from *The Buddy Deane Show* to coach his
cast and extras on such dance numbers as the
Dirty Boogie, the Roach and the Madison. The
pleasurable and relaxed experience made Ricki
feel as though she were on the set of an old Judy
Garland and Mickey Rooney MGM musical. In her
letters to home, Ricki described working on *Hairspray* to being at a really cool summer camp.

Several well-known performers—including Sonny
Bono, Pia Zadora and Ric Ocasek—were cast in

various roles. "I used Sonny Bono 'cause he's politically correct, and Debbie Harry 'cause huge
wigs look so good on her and she's so glamorous,"
said Waters. "As for Pia Zadora, she's everything
I believe in, and my kind of movie star. She's
smaller than Liz Taylor, cuter than the Chip-
munks, richer than Cher, and has better hairdos
than Farrah. What more could you ask for?" Waters also invited Buddy Deane and dancers from
the *The Buddy Deane Show* to play bit parts in
the movie. Taking a cue from the late, and highly
regarded, film director Alfred Hitchcock, who enjoyed popping up in cameo roles in his movies, Waters cast himself in *Hairspray,* playing a demented
psychiatrist who attempts electrical behavior mod-
ification on Ricki's character, Tracy.

Although the movie included several well-
known celebrities, there were people who disappointed Waters by turning down his request to
appear in *Hairspray.* "I also desperately wanted
Amy Carter for the film," revealed Waters. "My
ultimate casting choice would be Lana Turner, but
sadly there just wasn't a role for her in *Hairspray.*"

During the shoot, Ricki developed an immediate
rapport with Divine, who treated her like a daughter. "They called me the Baby Divine," said Ricki.
"To me, that's a great compliment."

Taking a paternal interest in Ricki, who was a newcomer, Divine also taught her how to walk in heels. Ricki later recalled a shaky moment during the shoot. She was standing on Eastern Avenue in an extremely tight-fitting dress that resembled the outfit Divine was also wearing, and was directed to walk alongside her costar. But thanks to her tight dress, Ricki had trouble moving her legs. After several missed takes, Divine finally did a shimmy, grabbed Ricki and dragged her with him. "Shake it, baby!" he implored. "Shake it!" On the next take, Ricki captured the walk perfectly, and even received a spontaneous round of applause from the crew.

"Ricki was delightful and I hate her. I got to admire her so much," Divine told *Interview* magazine.

Although Divine enjoyed working with Ricki, there were tense moments on the set during the first few days of shooting. Arriving on the set on the first day, Divine felt overlooked when he discovered that the well-known stars, who had considerably smaller roles in the movie than he was playing, were awarded their own private trailers, while he had to change in the men's general dressing room. Divine's discomfort at changing with the other actors wasn't based entirely on feeling that

he should've been given star treatment. Since
Hairspray was employing hundreds of extras, most
of whom had never worked on a film before, Divine
felt embarrassed having to change into women's
clothing in front of the gawking young adolescent
males who were used in the dance sequences.

After Divine complained about the oversight, he
was chagrined when he arrived for work on the
second day and learned that he still didn't have his
own trailer. Voicing his complaints in a stronger,
more effective manner, Divine was pleased when
he arrived to work on the third day and was escorted to his own private trailer.

From that point on, Divine's anger dissolved
and he was extremely relaxed during the shoot.
Waters was particularly impressed by the lively
performance Divine was delivering. "Divine
brings out my dialogue the way I like it," noted
Waters. "He fleshes out—literally—a character
better than anybody."

During the evenings, Waters screened his earlier
films for his young, curious performers. Waters,
however, made one exception. Ricki wasn't allowed to sit in on the screenings. "I didn't want it
to change her opinion of me," he explained.

Between camera setups, Divine sat with the
young stars and shared amusing stores about his

life on the road as a disco recording star. Ricki was
particularly enchanted by Divine's stories. Occasionally, Divine also performed Sixties dances that
he remembered and the young stars, including
Ricki, would work feverishly to imitate his moves.
After screening Divine's work in Waters's earlier
films, where he was attacked by a fifteen-foot lob-
ster in one movie, and sampled dog poop in another, the kids were filled with a multitude of
questions regarding the authenticity of Divine's
performance.

"Did you really eat dog poop?" they'd ask in-
credulously. Usually, Divine enjoyed answering
their questions, but when they became too personal, he'd good-naturedly respond, "None of your
business!" and change the subject.

Although Ricki wasn't required to do anything
with dog poop in *Hairspray,* there were moments
where she found herself challenged by some of Waters's more bizarre touches. In one scene, which
was later cut, live cockroaches crawled over Ricki's
back. In another scene, as her character was
smooching in a dark alley, a rat suddenly raced
across her foot. Without missing a beat, Ricki,
staying in character, chased the rat away with a
flick of her foot. Discussing the offbeat scenes,
Ricki said, "I didn't care. I didn't even mind hav-

ing a rat sit on my foot. John is a man I trust implicitly."

But Ricki didn't look back favorably on a scene where she was required to flick her tongue across a television screen showing St. Gerard's image. After *Hairspray* was released, Ricki recalled, "People come and say it was their favorite shot in the movie." With a frown, she added, "It tasted of Windex."

As shooting progressed, Waters found himself more pleased with Ricki, both personally and professionally, than he'd originally anticipated or hoped. "Ricki brought to my films, for the first time—for the *very* first time—some semblance of normalcy. Which I think people found very refreshing," he said. "She has an incredible natural charm to make people like her. Everybody likes her."

With more money allotted to shoot *Hairspray* than his earlier works, Waters felt a responsibility to bring it in on budget. Consequently, Waters found himself having to pull in a tight rein when it looked as if things were wavering off course. "I don't think I'm a dictator on the set, though I like to keep control, if only for business reasons," he said. "It's frightening how costs have escalated over the years. I made *Pink Flamingos* for twelve thousand dollars. *Hairspray* cost closer to two-point-seven million!"

Waters also realized he was working on a much bigger scale when it suddenly started to pour during the filming of an outdoor, on-location sequence. "I knew it was a big-budget movie when it started raining and an assistant handed me a plastic raincoat," he said.

After several weeks of shooting, Waters suddenly noticed that Ricki was losing weight. Taking his young leading lady aside, he urged her not to alter her eating habits until the movie was completed. Recalling the incident, he jokingly commented to a reporter, "We had to force-feed her milk shakes so she wouldn't be coming around a corner twenty pounds lighter than the last scene."

By the end of the shoot, Ricki felt as if she had made several new friends, including Waters. "John is so smart," she said. "I have so much respect for him. He's my role model, period."

With her first movie finished at the end of August, Ricki returned to her parents' home in New York. The following February, *Hairspray* enjoyed a national release and America was introduced to a new star, Ricki Lake.

4

"Public Accolades"

Hairspray's first public screening was at the Miami Film Festival. Soon after, the movie premiered in Baltimore, in February 1988. Ricki looked forward to the premiere because it was the first time she'd been reunited with cast and crew. Everyone from the film who attended the premiere complimented Ricki on her new figure. Since completing filming in August 1987, she'd lost thirty-five pounds.

Meanwhile, dozens of photographers and television news crews were on hand to cover the premiere. Ricki was filled with smiles as she graciously posed for the photographers, flattered by the attention. Baltimore native Ric Ocasek, who had a cameo role in *Hairspray* as a spaced-out beatnik, was accompanied by his beautiful girlfriend, actress/model Paulina Porizkova. Awed by

the glitter of the premiere, Ricki considered taking
Divine's advice to keep a show business diary,
which she attempted. But when Ricki re-read it a
week later, she decided her prose was sentimental
drivel and she trashed the diary. "I should've
known he was pulling my leg," said Ricki.

Movie critics were effusive in their praise of
Ricki's debut film performance.

"No Molly Ringwald needed; Lake is the dream
image of every girl who has ever craved that eighth
Twinkie." *Time Magazine*.

"Ricki Lake cheerfully comes out a winner.
Much like her chubby-but-chic character, who
makes it to the top through sheer willful personal-
ity and nonstop dancepower. We'll take her over
Jennifer Grey and Jennifer Beals any day." *Los
Angeles Weekly*.

"Ricki Lake may not look like Paulina Porizkova, but in Waters's eyes she's clearly possessed
of a sense of *joie de vivre* that even that celebrated
fashion model would envy. Consequently, you not
only find yourself cheering her on as she overpow-
ers the competition, you actually *believe* her rival's
beau would find her preferable. She's the hottest
girl in Baltimore." *Los Angeles Herald Examiner*.

Although Ricki was elated by her notices, she
also found herself feeling apprehensive. "It was

pretty scary," she said. "The reviews for *Hair-spray* were so great. I don't see how I'll be able to top myself."

In the meantime, on the heels of *Hairspray*'s national release, Ricki found herself the hottest girl in America. Suddenly, people were approaching her on the street and complimenting her performance in the movie. When Ricki dined in restaurants, other patrons shyly approached the table requesting her autograph. Initially, Ricki didn't quite trust the attention she was getting. "It's got to be a joke, right?" she said. "I mean, me? A movie star? C'mon!" Ricki's self-effacing humility was one of the qualities that attracted fans to her.

One afternoon, while Ricki was window-shopping in Manhattan, a young man politely approached Ricki, introduced himself and handed her a dozen long-stem roses. "It was so sweet," recalled Ricki with a wide smile. "I just stood there in shock."

Before *Hairspray* even premiered, Ricki landed roles in two other feature films. She had a minor role in *Working Girl,* a Twentieth Century Fox comedy that starred Harrison Ford, Melanie Griffith and Sigourney Weaver. A highlight for Ricki, who played a bridesmaid, was dancing with Harrison Ford during a wedding reception sequence. "He's even better-looking in person," she noted.

After completing her role on *Working Girl,* Ricki was cast as Pia Dianne van Cusso in *Cookie,* a gangster comedy produced by Lorimar Film Entertainment, which also starred Emily Lloyd and Peter Falk. Director Susan Seidelman, who had directed·Madonna's first film, *Desperately Seeking Susan,* sought Ricki for the role in *Cookie* after catching the talented young actress's performance in the coming attractions for *Hairspray.* Shooting began on January 4th in New York City. "It's a good supporting role," said Ricki, "which is a nice switch from *Hairspray,* where I was the main focus. I play Emily's best friend—we're pals—so the whole film isn't riding on my performance."

With three major films under her belt within the course of six months, Ricki said, "It's a fat girl's fairy tale. My weight is what makes me different from all the blue-eyed blondes."

The attention Ricki received from *Hairspray* also affected her romantic life. Although she wasn't seriously dating anyone, Ricki said she met a lot of guys through the movie. "I'm so happy," she said at the time. Ricki didn't even mind that some of her suitors were initially attracted to her because of *Hairspray.* "It's tough sometimes to know whether it's me they like or that I'm in the movies, but right now I'm not too worried. I'm just concentrating on having some fun for a change," she said.

The press, meanwhile, was anxious to question Ricki about her career goals as an actress and how she thought she'd fare landing future film roles. "I hope *Hairspray* will be a breakthrough," she said. "But I'm not out to be like a Robert DeNiro, lose fifty pounds and be anorexic."

Three weeks after *Hairspray*'s premiere, Ricki received shocking news. On March 7th, Divine died in his sleep during a visit to Los Angeles, where he was taping a guest appearance on the Fox television series *Married . . . With Children.* "He was an inspiration and my role model," said Ricki, speaking of Divine's death. "I was lucky I got to work with him and I'll miss him terribly."

That summer, Ricki landed her fourth film role as Donna, a pregnant teenager, in the dramatic feature *Last Exit to Brooklyn,* produced by Cinecom, which also starred Jennifer Jason Leigh. Set in the early fifties, *Last Exit to Brooklyn,* a dark story with several violent scenes, was shot mostly on location in the Red Hook section of Brooklyn over the course of ten weeks. Unlike her earlier films, which were mostly comedic, Ricki was called upon to turn in a dramatic performance for this one. "It was a tough film for me," said Ricki, "even though I'm one of the luckier characters. I only get raped once and then I get pregnant." While critics were

divided in their opinions of the film, Ricki generally received positive notices for her performance.
"Ricki Lake is radiant," wrote *Los Angeles Weekly*.

Meanwhile, John Waters had his own take on
Ricki's increasing popularity. "She's twenty years
old and drag queens are doing her. That's a star,"
he noted with pride.

As far as her film roles were concerned, Ricki
felt grateful that she wasn't being typecast as an
overweight actress. "*Hairspray* has opened a lot of
doors for me," she said. "They're not seeing me as
just *the fat girl*. They're seeing me in other roles
and making creative choices about using me. It's
great."

Although the roles Ricki was being cast in
weren't as big as the one she played in *Hairspray*,
it didn't bother her. "Acting is a blast!" she said.
"I don't care about the size of the role or the
money. I just want the phone to keep ringing!"

Soon after completing her role in *Last Exit to
Brooklyn*, Ricki had a chance to play a lead character again. She was cast as Grace Johnson in *Babycakes*, a TV movie that was loosely based on a 1985
German film, *Sugarbaby*, that focused on an attractive overweight woman trying to find love. Co-
incidentally, the role, at least in spirit, was similar
to Tracy Turnblad from *Hairspray*. "The role re-

quired little acting," Ricki noted. "Basically, I'm Tracy."

Babycakes producer Diana Kerwew, who was a fan of Ricki's work, said, "This is not a typical love story," she said. "And Ricki's an improbable heroine, but the audience will love her. She is so adorable."

After playing two characters who were specifically created as overweight, Ricki said with a good-natured laugh, "My plan is to define the role of fat-girl-as-heroine. I'm going to make fat fashionable again."

Playing opposite Ricki in *Babycakes* was Craig Sheffer, who later starred as Brad Pitt's older brother in Robert Redford's *A River Runs through It*. "Craig is such a hunk," Ricki confessed. "And we kiss in this movie constantly." Frustrated by the relative tameness of the TV movie's romantic scenes, especially after having appeared in *Last Exit to Brooklyn*, Ricki approached the producers with suggestions on how to make things more interesting. "I said, 'Can't we add some originality? Like, can I suck his toes?' But they wouldn't go for that."

Babycakes also required Ricki to appear in a bathtub scene, a prospect she found more frightening than having roaches crawl all over her back in *Hairspray*. Speaking about the bathtub scene,

Ricki said, "I almost turned down this movie because of that one scene. I was so petrified doing
it." Ever the trouper, though, Ricki saw a bright
side to the situation. "If I can do this, I can do
anything," she told herself before filming the
scene. *Babycakes,* which was described as "a romantic comedy," was broadcast in the United
States on CBS on, appropriately, Valentine's Day
1989.

Just as they were with Ricki's earlier work, critics were supportive of her latest venture. In a review of *Babycakes,* the *New York Daily News*
wrote, "Lake has an offbeat style, and offers a re-
spite from all the perfect females on TV." It was
an observation that warmed Ricki's heart. She was
succeeding in a business where "blue-eyed,
shapely blondes" usually got the attention.

In the months following the release of *Hairspray,*
Ricki wasn't in any hurry to make big changes in
her personal life. Too many things were happening
in her career. With her busy workload, Ricki enjoyed returning home to the security of her loving
parents and sister. "So many things have been
happening," she said, "I think it's a good idea for
me to have a stable home life. It keeps me
normal."

By the end of the year, however, Ricki realized

that if she wanted to continue landing film roles on a consistent basis, she'd have to be where the majority of movies were being shot, Hollywood. "My only fear is that this is one of those success stories that lasts twenty-two minutes. I've got big plans for myself. Very big plans," she said. Rather than placing herself on a strict diet, and potentially making herself more eligible for a broader range of the film roles that were available in New York City, Ricki realized she'd never be model-thin, so why not try Hollywood just as she was? "As long as I'm healthy and happy, who cares if I'm a little overweight?" she asked. "Don't think of me as fat. Think of me as larger than life."

Soon after arriving in Hollywood, Ricki was quickly besieged with offers to star in television series. After sifting through the dozens of pilot scripts that were submitted to her agent, Ricki finally selected a series tentatively titled *Starting Now* that was produced by Paramount. *Starting Now* was similar in premise to the popular sixties sitcom *That Girl,* which starred Marlo Thomas as a struggling actress. *Starting Now* was tailored specially around Ricki's unique talents. Over the course of six months, Ricki met regularly with the writers who were scripting the pilot for *Starting Now,* offering ideas and suggestions. Ricki loved traveling to the Paramount lot and meeting with

the writers. On the busy lot there was a sense of
history; some of Ricki's favorite television programs as a child had been filmed at Paramount,
including *The Brady Bunch.*

In the pilot script that was shot, Ricki played a
production assistant on a children's program who
desperately wanted to succeed as an actress.
Henry Winkler, who formerly starred as Fonzie on
the seventies sitcom *Happy Days,* directed the
pilot, which was taped on a Paramount Studios
soundstage in front of a studio audience, in the
spring of '89.

As Ricki waited to hear if the series would be
picked up by CBS, she tried to adjust to her new
life in Hollywood. Everywhere Ricki turned, it
seemed she was running into celebrities. She spot-
ted Tom Hanks, her favorite actor, at a restaurant
where she was dining. On another occasion she entered a trendy Beverly Hills restaurant and encountered Lois Smith, a powerful publicist who
represented such high-profile clients as Robert
Redford, Sean Penn and Cher. Whenever she ate
out, Ricki was well aware that the vast majority of
servers who took her food order were hoping for
the big break that would place them in her position. Conscious of her good fortune, Ricki said, "I
don't think I've paid my dues enough. I've never
been a waitress and that's like a prerequisite."

That same spring, Ricki was asked to perform a musical number at the Academy Awards with several other young performers who were billed as "Hollywood's new faces." It was a dream come true for Ricki, who'd have plenty of opportunity to see her favorite movie stars in person. But even better, she was going to be a part of the ceremonies. Rather than feeling nervous about the prospect of performing on a show that was broadcast live all over the world, Ricki was excited. "I had to do this big number in front of two billion people," she said. "I was the only one who wasn't nervous. I remember Chad Lowe was shaking and freaking out. I was like, 'It's gonna be okay. It's no big deal.'"

After performing her number, near the beginning of the show, Ricki took a seat in the star-filled auditorium. "That was the *greatest* night of my life!" she said. In addition to spotting Meg Ryan, one of her favorite actresses, Ricki sat next to a legend, Lucille Ball, the reigning "queen of television comedy." (It turned out to be Ball's last public appearance. Shortly after she appeared at the Academy Awards, Lucille Ball passed away at Cedar-Sinai Hospital in Los Angeles.) At one point, Ricki locked eyes with Tom Cruise, who flashed his dazzling trademark smile her way. Moments later, Cruise approached Ricki and introduced himself. "He kissed me!" she said. To her stunned surprise, Cruise revealed he was a big fan of her work and said he hoped to work with her someday. As if things couldn't get any better, Cruise introduced Ricki to Dustin Hoffman, his co-star from *Rainman*.

In May, CBS announced its fall season schedule. Missing from the lineup was Ricki's proposed series, *Starting Now*. It was the first major rejection Ricki had suffered since moving to Los Angeles, and it stung. Ricki was also bewildered by *Starting Now*'s absence from the fall schedule. Based on the favorable responses she'd been hearing from executives at the network, Ricki had had high hopes for the series.

Soon after, Ricki received word from an old friend that raised her spirits. John Waters was directing a new movie and he'd written a part especially for her.

5

"Cry-Baby"

In the summer of 1989, Ricki prepared to film her second movie with John Waters, *Cry-Baby*. "It's a musical about juvenile delinquents in 1954," said John Waters. "A good girl from the right side of the tracks falls in love with a bad boy." Waters wrote the movie as a comic send-up of the black-and-white juvenile delinquent films that showed at drive-in theaters in the mid-fifties. "I always wanted to be a juvenile delinquent when I was growing up, but my parents wouldn't let me," said Waters. "So I'm finally getting my chance."

There were several similarities between *Hairspray* and *Cry-Baby*. Just as he had done with *Hairspray*, Waters focused on a period right before a major social change took place. He'd set *Hairspray* in 1962, shortly before President Kennedy was assassinated and before the Beatles enjoyed worldwide fame. "I've always been intrigued with things that happen right before something major occurs culturally, and *Cry-Baby* takes place right before rock 'n' roll started," he explained. Like *Hairspray,* Waters's newest movie also relied heavily on music from the mid-fifties to help evoke a mood. "The music we researched should tell as much of the story as the dialogue," he noted. In *Hairspray* Waters spread a message about racial tolerance. "If I was forced to be socially redeeming, I'd guess I'd say with *Cry-Baby* we're giving a warning against conforming," he revealed. Both films also featured Ricki Lake in a key role.

Based on his positive experience working with Ricki on *Hairspray,* Waters had been anxious to find a new role for her in his next film. "Ricki Lake is someone I'd like to have in every one of my films," he said. "She's a real sweetheart." Although Waters knew he wanted to include Ricki in the film, he said that while writing the screenplay for *Cry-Baby* he'd tried to avoid envisioning specific actors in the new roles he was creating until the characters were fully developed. "I keep a folder of people I'd like to work with, and I'll always refer to that and try to work from it when I first think about casting," he explained. Naturally, Ricki was at the top of the list.

*   *   *

Cry-Baby had one of the most eclectic casts to
come out of a Hollywood studio. In the lead title
role, Waters cast Johnny Depp, star of the popular
Fox TV crime series *21 Jump Street*. "Johnny
hated being a teen idol," said Waters, "and I told
him the best way to get rid of an image . . . any
image . . . is to make fun of it. I think he was very
brave to take this part because, first off, he told me
that it was the most peculiar script he had ever
seen, and by portraying Cry-Baby, he's right out
there making fun of himself."

"*Cry-Baby* came along at a good time for me,"
said Johnny Depp. "I had been looking at film
ideas for a while and was getting disillusioned.
Most of what I read was flat, just shlock." Depp
felt particularly discouraged that most of the
scripts mirrored the role he played on *21 Jump
Street*. So when Waters approached him about *Cry-
Baby* it was an opportune moment. "John first
sent me a letter and then we talked a bit and met,
and then he gave me a script. I was so excited because not only was it really funny, but it made fun
of all those cliches and sensitive-hero roles I had
been reading for so long."

Waters recalled his first introduction to Depp at
an office on the Universal Studio lot. "Johnny
came into this lovely Hollywood office in complete

rags," said Waters. Intrigued by the young star's attire, Waters proceeded to chat with him about the movie and the role he was up for. "In the middle of the meeting he looked at me and gave me a sneer," continued Waters. It was a gesture that harkened back to Ricki Lake's first meeting with Waters, when she'd candidly asked him about his red eyes. Ricki's candidness led to the starring role in *Hairspray,* and it looked as if Depp's sneer promised to do the same for him in *Cry-Baby.* "At that moment, I realized he would do just fine," noted Waters. "He understood the whole plot of the film." Before the meeting's conclusion, Waters and Depp discovered they had quite a bit in common, including the fact that they both owned paintings by serial killer John Wayne Gacy and that they shared a mutual admiration for Pia Zadora.

Soon after the meeting, Depp signed a contract for his first starring role in a major motion picture, one that promised to broaden the image that had surrounded him since starring on *21 Jump Street.* "One of the reasons I did *Cry-Baby* was so I could make fun of this image that has been shoved down America's throats [about me]: teen heartthrob, bad boy, young rebel, all those filthy little labels for this manufactured image that I didn't manufacture," he said. "If there's a statement to be made from the movie—and I don't think John intended any statement—it's that what you would normally judge as one thing is not necessarily what it is. What's that old thing about 'don't judge a book by its cover'? It's as simple as that."

In a supporting role as Wanda Woodward, the sexiest girl in town, Waters cast Traci Lords, who had previously appeared in seventy-five porno films, starting when she was fourteen years old. Commenting on Lords, Waters said, "She obviously wasn't just another porno star. I wouldn't want any other porno stars in my films. They're a dime a dozen. She was something special. She's Jessica Rabbit—and I mean that in the best way."

Making her movie debut as Traci's mother in *Cry-Baby* was Patricia Hearst, who first entered the national consciousness when she was kidnapped in the early seventies by a terrorist group and then later renounced her wealthy family, which owned a publishing conglomerate, after being brainwashed. Waters said he didn't have any difficulty persuading Hearst to appear in his movie. "It was easy because I knew Patty. She knew I was her fan. I met her at Cannes after seeing the Paul Schrader film *Patty Hearst,* which I loved. But I'd also been at her trial for weeks at a time, and was obsessed by her case for years. I told her that *Patty Hearst* made me believe she was

innocent for the first time, which, when you think
about it, is sort of a backhanded compliment, but
I think she liked that. . . . Her kids liked *Hairspray*.
Patty has a sense of humor," said Waters. Meanwhile David Nelson, who'd starred with his family
in *The Adventures of Ozzie and Harriet,* was cast
to play Hearst's husband.

Waters also cast singer Joey Heatherton to play
a minister's wife who spoke in tongues. "Joey was
a little bit from another planet, but I've been on
other planets," he said. "She was sweet, and
everybody liked her and was protective of her, and
she was completely professional. She had a lot of
pocketbooks, and maybe that was weird."

Referring to the diverse assortment of people assembled for his newest movie, including Willem
Dafoe, an Oscar-nominated actor, Waters said, "I
like to mix and match. I think all movies should
be stews. I like all kinds of ingredients. There are
certain people I'd never put in a film, people like
Zsa Zsa Gabor, who're really bad . . . people whom
you'd think I'd like and you'd be wrong. It's a thin
line." Waters also compared the unique casting in
Cry-Baby to a fun party, where you meet a lot of
interesting, different people and hate to leave
when it's over. "I hate parties where everybody's
the same. I like it when each person is completely
different and you know what it is and it's confusing, and that to me is sexy," he said.

Notably missing from *Cry-Baby*'s cast was Waters's longtime friend, Divine. While writing the
script, Waters revealed he'd been haunted by Divine's voice. Concerned that people would speculate on which character Divine would've played in
Waters's first movie since the talented character
actor's death, he took pains to rewrite the script
over and over, until none of the characters could
be interpreted as one that Divine would've played.

After reading *Cry-Baby*'s screenplay, Ricki observed, "It's sort of an updated *West Side Story*.
It's also a comedy. So, it's got everything in it, including me.

"When I first read *Cry-Baby*, I loved the idea
that it was a musical," she added. "With so few
made anymore, I knew that if anyone could pull it
off, John could. No matter what size the role, and
no matter what I would have to do, I would do it
just to work with John again. I couldn't wait to get
back to Baltimore."

Ricki was also looking forward to playing Pepper
Walker, Cry-Baby's teenage sister, who's constantly pregnant. "She's a girl who likes being
knocked up and plays the drums in her spare
time," noted Ricki. "It's a real stretch for me."

Although *Cry-Baby* was a musical, Ricki's vocal
talents weren't required. "I don't get to sing in

any of my films," she said. But as Ricki delved into her new role, she felt an optimism about her acting talent that she hadn't experienced in her earlier film roles. "It's the first project I've ever been on that I felt I was going to be really, really good," she explained.

With shooting scheduled to begin in early summer in Baltimore, Ricki packed her bags, made arrangements for a friend to care for her two Blue Russian cats, Annie and Molly, and caught an early morning plane out of Los Angeles.

Before shooting started on *Cry-Baby*, Waters paid a visit to Divine's grave at Prospect Hill Cemetery. He was accompanied by Johnny Depp. Divine's gravesite was located near a cluster of trees. His headstone read simply, "Harris Glenn Milstead— Divine." Waters revealed to Depp that when Divine worked as a hairdresser in his younger days, he used to steal flowers off the graves at Prospect Hill Cemetery for his dinner parties. After their quiet visit at the cemetery, Waters took Depp on a tour of his favorite part of Baltimore, otherwise known as "Pigtown." "Which is this section with all row houses," said Depp. "People just hang out on their doorsteps. In summer they bring their TVs and their chairs outside. The women will be in their bras."

When the cast of *Cry-Baby* gathered to meet on the first day of shooting, Ricki said, "Divine's presence and spirit was missed, but John said he had everyone in the cast except Baby Jessica, who fell in the well, and Mother Teresa, which is true."

Although Ricki was happy to be reunited with several crew members who had also worked on *Hairspray,* and enjoyed catching up with them, it was a different story for Traci Lords. A newcomer to a John Waters movie, Traci said she felt apprehensive meeting everyone for the first time. "I was worried how the other actors would react to me," she revealed. However, Traci's nervousness dissolved that evening after cast and crew gathered at a nearby bar to get acquainted. "Tequilla opened up a lot of minds," she noted.

During the shoot, Patricia Hearst had a surprising realization. Other cast members had had a brush with the law. Right before the filming Johnny Depp got arrested for assaulting a hotel security guard. (Depp was later cleared of all charges, received an absolute discharge and experienced no negative effects as a result of the publicity surrounding the incident.)

As shooting progressed, Ricki received a new, affectionate nickname from Waters. "John called me Divith, half Divine and half Edith Massey [who'd also starred in Waters's earlier films, and had died in 1984]," she revealed. "He padded my stomach to make me look like Divine, twenty months pregnant, and dressed me like Edith," said Ricki. Unlike her work on *Hairspray,* however, where a disheartened Ricki watched as her hair was trimmed, dyed and teased, she got to wear a hairpiece in *Cry-Baby*.

During the shoot, Ricki developed a close friendship with Depp that would carry over after *Cry-Baby* was completed. They'd spend their time laughing and being silly between shots. Depp also observed that Ricki was one of the most affectionate people he'd ever met. "Ricki's like Cupid," he said. "She's a little love thing. She always wants to hug and love. We felt close right away."

Cry-Baby was filmed on a budget between eight and eleven million dollars. It was Waters's first big-scale, big-budget motion picture. He received financing from Ron Howard's Imagine Films at Universal Pictures. "John has a bigger budget and has more pressure because of the big studio," said Ricki at the time. "But it's still John Waters," she added for fans of Waters's earlier works who feared he might compromise his artistic integrity now that he had aligned himself with a major Hollywood studio.

"I think *Cry-Baby* will look exactly like an eight-million-dollar John Waters movie," the director said. Comparing the shoot to his earlier, low-budget movies, particularly before *Hairspray,* he added, "We had heat this time. We had running water. Those are the major stylistic differences—toilets!"

One stunt that was expensive to produce involved Ricki's character, Pepper. While Ricki, who was wearing a form-fitting, accordian-pleated dress, was squeezed into the backseat of an old car, with a huge, pillowed stomach, her character suddenly went into labor. Meanwhile, Johnny Depp was secured to the roof of the car, while a game of *chicken* was suspensefully being played on a highway at high speed. "I know this is the most unattractive I've ever looked!" Ricki pointed out. Nevertheless, Ricki was having so much fun in the role that she paid little attention to how she looked, and focused instead on Waters's steady direction.

After several weeks of shooting at night, *Cry-Baby* reverted to a daytime schedule, complete with early morning casting calls. One sequence was filmed at the Franklin School in Baltimore. At the crack of dawn, a bus picked up the bleary-eyed actors who were scheduled to be on the set, including Ricki, and dropped them off at the school in time to make their six-thirty A.M. call. As expected,

the sight of actors dressed in fifties-style costumes
drew stares from neighbors who lived near the
Franklin School. "It was like a traveling circus,"
said Waters. "We just pulled up by the caravans
and let the lunatics out."

During the course of the shoot, Waters, Depp
and Traci Lords celebrated birthdays. "For Traci's
twenty-first birthday we had three cakes, a case of
champagne and all the weirdos of the world," said
Iggy Pop, who had a featured role in *Cry-Baby*.

Meanwhile, Johnny Depp revealed that he had
"a very Baltimore birthday." That summer, a
scandal involving actor Rob Lowe, who was shown
in a home video having sexual relations with a
woman while a male friend watched, was being cir-
culated all over the country, eventually making its
way to Baltimore, where it was given to Depp as a
gift. He also received a color-illustrated medical
text on human deformities from Waters, as well as
an audiotape of Jim Jones's last sermon in Jones-
town, where he directed his followers to drink
Kool-Aid that had been laced with lethal poison.
Sharing his impressions of Waters, whom Depp became good friends with during the shoot, Depp
said, "What shocked me about John Waters was
that he was so accessible and normal."

As the shoot drew to a close, Ricki approached
Depp for career advice. Although she enjoyed star-

ring in movies, Ricki feared the work wasn't steady enough and wondered if she should consider television. Depp, who was anxious to break away from the grind of a weekly television series, advised Ricki to continue working in film.

The following April, *Cry-Baby* was released nationwide to mixed reviews and suffered a lukewarm response at the box office. Reflecting on the disinterest of the American viewing public in his latest film, and with a nod to Divine's absence in the movie, Waters said, "I thought I could trick them with Johnny Depp. But they smelled a rat— me."

Meanwhile, soon after *Cry-Baby*'s release, Ricki decided to steer her career in a different direction. Ignoring Depp's well-meaning advice, Ricki focused her attention on television.

6

"China Beach"

In 1989, Ricki placed a hefty down payment on her first home, a three-bedroom fixer-upper country house nestled in the Hollywood Hills, valued at seven hundred fifty thousand dollars. In typical Hollywood fashion, the house also had a spacious swimming pool. Ricki purchased the house partly as an investment. But the extra rooms were for when her parents and sister were in town to visit. In the meantime, Ricki shared the space with her two cats and a new addition to her family, a cockapoo she adopted named Dudley.

That same year, Ricki finally became a true devotee of the Southern California lifestyle when she bought her first car. Initially, she considered buying a BMW. But with a large house payment to cover every month, Ricki lowered her sights considerably. "I ended up with a Honda," she said.

Ricki's social life was also on an upswing. Since moving to Los Angeles earlier in the year, she'd made several new friends, including her costar from *Cry-Baby,* Johnny Depp, whom she affectionately referred to as her big brother. Finding dates to accompany her to Hollywood events also wasn't a problem for Ricki, whose winning personality drew men to her.

The only thing missing to make Ricki's life truly carefree was a steady paycheck. Once Ricki returned from the *Cry-Baby* shoot in Baltimore, she found it difficult lining up the next movie gig. Frustrated by the lack of support she was receiving from the talent agency that represented her, Ricki decided to make a switch. Soon after, she received an offer to appear as a semi-regular on the ABC drama series *China Beach.*

The critically acclaimed series, which had been running on ABC for two seasons, focused on the lives of women at a military base during the Vietnam War. Dana Delany, who played the lead character, Nurse Colleen McMurphy, was awarded an Emmy as Best Actress in a Drama Series. Ricki, who had never seen *China Beach,* was apprehensive about making the switch to television. The disappointment of not seeing her sitcom, *Starting Over,* picked up by CBS was still fresh in her mind. Having appeared in several high-profile films,

Ricki also worried that a role on a television series might lower her value as a film actress. But the new agency representing Ricki urged her to seriously consider accepting the part on *China Beach,* and promised that she'd have plenty of time to appear in movies when the series went on hiatus for three months in the spring and early summer.

Wanting to keep her options open, Ricki met with the executive producers of *China Beach.* Sitting across from Ricki in a comfortable Hollywood office, the producers described Holly Pelligrino, the character they envisioned her playing. Like Ricki, Holly was fun-spirited. She was a "donut dolly" who participated in variety shows that entertained the troops. After hearing the producers' plans for the character in the coming season, Ricki left the meeting feeling intrigued by the prospects of appearing on a dramatic television series. Giving careful thought to the character the producers described to her, Ricki said, "We're one and the same. Her biggest asset is to flirt. And that's my favorite thing to do." Ricki also considered the opportunity she'd have to play the same character for a sustained period of time, giving her the chance to explore new nuances to Holly's personality on a weekly basis. "Holly's well aware of why she's in Vietnam. She's a smart girl, but she's the baby of all those there. Her perky energy makes the guys happy. She reminds them of home. But she also grates on McMurphy's nerves, which is great because we have a little conflict."

Sitting alone in her new home, Ricki weighed the positives and negatives of taking the role. On the positive side, by joining the show, Ricki reasoned, she'd be bringing a lighter edge to the often-dark series. Since *China Beach* didn't film year-round, she'd still be able to accept at least one role a year in a film (so far, she'd been averaging at least two roles a year). Holly was an entertainer, which would give Ricki a chance to do something she'd never been able to do in films: sing. A role on a television series would also give her more exposure, thereby potentially making it easier for her to land new film roles. "The cool people saw *Hairspray*," she observed, "but everyone who has a TV set sees *China Beach*."

Being completely honest with herself, Ricki also realized that it wasn't until the last couple of years that she had even considered having a career in films. Prior to *Hairspray*, television had always been her first love. "I never saw movies when I was young," she said. "I always wanted to be on television [beginning with her dream to take over the role of Cindy on *The Brady Bunch*]. I was the oldest sister in my family, but I wanted to be the youngest child on television." Finally, the steady paycheck Ricki would receive from *China Beach* would ease her mind at the beginning of every month when her house payment was due.

When it came to weighing the negatives, Ricki quickly realized the positive advantages of appearing on *China Beach* far outweighed them. Picking up the phone, she directed her agents to make a deal with the executive producers.

Ricki's agents negotiated a lucrative contract with *China Beach* that guaranteed her a certain number of episodes during the coming season as a semi-regular cast member. "If the show is renewed for next season, I'll be a regular," she said. "That would be great. I'm proud to be on the show and love the show and the security of having a job to come back to."

China Beach was primarily filmed in two places. The interior scenes were shot at the Warner Brothers studio in Burbank, California. The exterior scenes were shot at Indian Dunes, which was a dense, wooded area several miles outside of Los Angeles. Several years earlier, the television series *M*A*S*H* also shot its exterior scenes in the same place. It was also the same area where the fatal helicopter crash on *The Twilight Zone* movie occurred, taking several lives, including those of character actor Vic Morrow and two Vietnamese children. *China Beach* cast-mate Marg Helenberger, who played K.C., a world-weary prostitute, dubbed the area "Hellhole" because of its miserable conditions. Since Indian Dunes was essentially in the desert, temperatures would often rise above a hundred degrees in the summer. During the evening, in the fall and winter months, they'd sometimes drop down to thirty degrees. Meanwhile, *China Beach*'s beach scenes were shot at Zuma.

When things were running relatively smoothly, the cast would receive a new script a week before it was scheduled to be filmed. By then, the producers had already worked out how many days it would take to film the episode and where specific episodes were going to be shot. Normally, one-hour dramas take nine days, at the most, to film. But for *China Beach,* ten days was usually the norm. The show's producers strived for authenticity in the look and feel of the series. As the season went on, the extra days used to film the episodes in the first few months put extra pressure on the cast and crew to get more work done in a shorter period of time. With the pace picking up to make up for the lost time, it wasn't unusual for actors to receive the next week's script while they were wrapping up the episode from the week before. Script changes were also frequent, and the cast would have to make adjustments for new scenes. Since it was a television series, there was also the added stress of filming a certain number of pages per day. Consequently, it wasn't unusual for the cast and crew to put in eighteen-hour days. For Ricki, who was used to filming two to three pages a day in movies, the quick pace on *China Beach* was going to be something new.

Since *China Beach* was set in the middle of a war, high-tech special effects were commonly utilized. Often, the realism depicted on *China Beach* raised the dander of the standards and practices department at ABC. John Sacret Young, *China Beach*'s executive producer and co-creator, said, "We're dealing with war, and the emotions of war. The broadcast standards attitude is that you can't show certain stuff on TV. Whereas we say: 'We're not trying to make a bloodbath here, but this is about war, this is triage, this is real.' For example, in one episode a nurse was working on a soldier whose foot came off with his boot. In the end we showed the boot with some blood, but no bones sticking out. . . . But we feel if we're not pushing the barriers a bit, we're not doing our job."

Ricki was immediately welcomed by the cast of *China Beach*. Nancy Giles, who played Frankie, had admired Ricki's work since she first saw her in *Hairspray*. Impressed by Ricki's dancing in the

film, Giles wanted to know more about how she
learned the dances, especially the Madison. Before
long, Ricki was teaching Giles the steps. To keep
themselves warm and entertained during long
shoots on cold nights in the Indian Dunes, Ricki
and Giles would sing well-known show tunes from
Broadway shows.

Ricki also became good friends with Brian Wimmer, who played Boonie. One personality trait that
both Ricki and Wimmer shared was flirting. In
September, Wimmer accompanied Ricki to the
Emmy Awards in Los Angeles. During the ceremony, Ricki and Wimmer had a great time, whis-
pering and laughing amongst themselves. *China
Beach*'s producers and writers immediately noticed the sizzling chemistry between Ricki and
Wimmer and decided to incorporate it into the
show. In a sweet episode that showcased the two
actors' talents, Ricki's character, Holly, told Boonie that she had fallen in love with him. Although
Boonie had a great deal of affection for Holly, he
didn't share the same feelings for her. By the end
of the episode, Holly and Wimmer had resolved to
remain good friends and the romantic angle was
dropped.

Meanwhile, as the season went on, it wasn't un-
common for Ricki to arrive at the studio proclaim-
ing to everyone in earshot, "I'm in love!" Between

icki and Darren Burrows became friends both on and off the
CRY-BABY set.

In high school, Ricki attended the Professional Children's School in Manhattan with Christian Slater.
RALPH DOMINGUEZ/ GLOBE PHOTOS

Ricki considers director John Waters her mentor and best friend.
JEAN ESTEB

cki with her younger sister Jennifer. "When we were growing up,
y sister and I looked alike, but we were complete opposites. I was
e outgoing one; she was the quieter one," said Ricki.

"I never believed in love at first sight until I met Rob," said Ricki.
JEAN ESTEB

Before Ricki lost weight she dressed in loose-fitting clothing. Self-conscious about shopping for clothes, she only took joy in buying hats.
JEAN ESTEB

icki with her sister Jennifer at a softball game. "I didn't know until
fter Ricki lost her weight how dissatisfied she was with herself,"
aid Jennifer. "I found out years later that she had a hat collection
ecause they were the only things that fit her. That was sad."
AN ESTEB

Ricki at the 1994 Daytime Emmys with Rob and her family. Ricki was nominated for Best TV Talk Show Host, but Oprah Winfrey won the award. (From left to right: Rob Sussman, Ricki Lake, her sister Jennifer, and parents, Jill and Barry)
JEAN ESTEB

arm messages from animal rights lovers and Ricki fans greeted
star outside the police station at her arraignment in 1994.
JRA CAVANAUGH/GLOBE PHOTOS

ki left her jail cell and headed directly for The Ed Sullivan Theater,
ere she was scheduled to make an appearance on *The Late Show*
ith David Letterman. "I'm happy to be out," she told reporters who
re standing outside the back door of the Criminal Courts Building
Manhattan.
LTER WEISSMAN/GLOBE PHOTOS

Ricki's involvement in an anti-fur demonstration organized by
PETA against designer Karl Lagerfeld landed her a night in jail.
When it was suggested by the media that Ricki participated in the
demonstration to get publicity for her talk show she responded,
"We're the number two show behind *Oprah*, we don't need any
more ratings!"

scenes, Ricki would rush to the phone to talk with her latest boyfriend. Usually, the romances were short-lived. Ricki, however, didn't remain despondent for long. Within days, she'd show up at the studio sharing stories about a new boyfriend she'd met and fallen for.

In each episode, *China Beach* often utilized between twenty and thirty extras, also known as "atmosphere players," because they appeared in the background, looking busy as the principal actors delivered their lines. Ricki was always cordial and friendly with the extras. Often, they'd ask Ricki about the films she'd appeared in, especially *Hairspray*.

Ricki particularly enjoyed working with Dana Delany. Comparing Delany to the nurse she played in the series, Ricki said, "McMurphy is moody and depressed. It's great to play opposite Dana. She has that edge that makes her endearing. Holly's happiness should make her endearing too. Her happiness is just the way she is. I'm pretty happy too. I think we're pretty similar. She knows more about Vietnam than I do, since I was born in 1968."

In September, Ricki threw herself a lavish party to celebrate her twenty-first birthday. Ricki enjoyed making plans for the party because it was the first she'd host in her new house. Friends she'd made on *China Beach,* as well as in the films she'd appeared in, were invited to the party. Several friends that Ricki had made during her first year in Hollywood were also sent invitations. Celebrities attending the high-spirited party included Marlee Matlin, Sarah Jessica Parker, and Brian Bloom (who had formerly appeared on Ricki's favorite daytime soap—Dusty). Friends of Ricki's, who knew that she was a big fan of the seventies sitcom *The Brady Bunch,* arranged for Eve Plumb, who played the middle sister, Jan, to attend the party. When Eve walked through the door, an elated Ricki dropped the conversation she was having with a cluster of friends and immediately screamed with excitement. "When she walked in I screamed in her face," Ricki said. "Scared her to death. She's my hero. She was like the best." Taking on the role of a giddy fan, Ricki shared her memories of favorite *Brady Bunch* episodes with Eve. She also told Eve how, as a child, she'd fantasized about taking over the role of the youngest Brady, Cindy. By the end of the night, Ricki and Eve had become good friends. During their conversation, Eve revealed that she was also a painter, and Ricki promised to attend the next showing of her work.

*   *   *

In November, Ricki found time to appear in her first Los Angeles theater production, Cynthia Heimel's *A Girl's Guide to Chaos,* which ran at the Tiffany Theatre on the Sunset Strip. "I'm not carrying the show," said Ricki. "It's a feature part—so I don't feel the pressure. Besides, it's a lot of fun, since my character, Lurene, is so different from me. She's a tough chick, married, with a kid, and tells it like it is to the play's older women, who are much more confused." Ricki also enjoyed delving into her character's unique personality. "I'm sweet and sugar-coated, feeling the need to please others, so I really admire Lurene," she said.

Meanwhile, Ricki also had plenty of room to show off her dramatic talents on *China Beach.* In one of the series' most controversial episodes, Holly had an abortion. The episode, which was told in flashback, explored Holly's feelings about a short-lived romance she'd had with a sailor that had fizzled. Pregnant and confused, Holly considered several options, such as raising the child alone, putting it up for adoption, or having an abortion. With K.C. and McMurphy's help, Holly eventually decided to have an abortion.

Ricki had mixed emotions about the episode. On one hand, she enjoyed the chance to play such weighty material. But she couldn't understand why Holly had to have an abortion. Curious to see if a change could be made, Ricki met personally with the writer responsible for the episode. "I said to the writer, 'Why? Why not have her lose the baby?' But they wanted to dramatize this issue and it was very hard."

After the episode was broadcast, Ricki received thousands of letters from viewers. A few of the more emotional letters were from women who'd been in a similar situation to Holly's and had also opted for an abortion. Some of the letter-writers expressed their regret at having made the decision to abort, while others wrote that the episode made them feel better about the heart-wrenching decision they'd made in their younger days. Meanwhile, Ricki also received letters from a fringe element who confused her with the character she played on the fictional television series. They chastised Ricki for the abortion and urged her to repent. "I had so much mail about that episode!" she said.

In another dramatic episode, Holly was shaken when evidence suggested that her friend Hang, played by Hauani Minn, was connected to the Viet Cong. Through her friendship with an unsuspecting Holly, Hang was getting information about where the "donut dollies" were going to entertain, and where American troops would be

fighting. She then leaked the information to her
relatives, who were working with the Viet Cong.
Midway through the episode, Holly's friend
Frankie was seriously wounded by a booby trap.
Although everyone else at the base suspected
Hang was behind Frankie's injury, Holly remained
loyal to her friend, refusing to believe that she was
responsible for setting the booby trap. Eventually,
it was revealed that Hang had been working with
the Viet Cong. At the show's poignant climax,
Ricki and Hauani sang "Blowin' in the Wind."
Moments later, a teary-eyed Holly watched as her
friend Hang was taken away by the military police.

In one of Ricki's first episodes, Holly organized
a Miss China Beach contest, much to the dismay of
Nurse McMurphy, who felt beauty pageants were
trivial and belittled women.

In another episode, Ricki participated in a cover
version of Aretha Franklin's hit "Think" with several other cast-mates, led by Nancy Giles, who
sang lead vocal.

Impressed by *China Beach*'s unwavering quality,
Ricki became one of the show's biggest boosters.
She appeared regularly on TV talk shows promot-
ing it. In hindsight, it also became clear to her why
her sitcom *Starting Now,* wasn't picked up by
CBS; she was supposed to be on *China Beach.*

"Had it worked out, I wouldn't be in *China Beach*," she reflected. "I'm happy now that I took the role."

Unfortunately, ABC wasn't as pleased with *China Beach* as Ricki was. In March, the show was suddenly placed on hiatus and replaced with a new drama series, *Equal Justice*, which focused on a group of Los Angeles defense attorneys. Dana Delany worked tirelessly behind the scenes, campaigning to rescue the series. She met with ABC programming executives and pleaded with them not to cancel it, citing its critical acclaim amongst fans and TV critics, as well as the show's success in its Wednesday night time period (*China Beach* usually won the slot). "Before this show people didn't know there were women in Vietnam. I didn't," said Delany. (But ABC executives remained noncommittal regarding the show's future. Out of ninety-six television series broadcast that season in prime-time, *China Beach* ranked forty-six.)

Two days before ABC would unveil its new fall schedule, *China Beach* executive producer John Sacret Young still hadn't received word on the show's fate. Although it was a Saturday, Young expected to hear from ABC at any time and stayed near his telephone, hoping to hear positive news. Delany kept Young company, lending much-needed emotional support. Late that afternoon, Young finally received a call from a high-ranking ABC executive. *China Beach* had received a reprieve and would appear on the network's fall schedule. "John was ecstatic," said Delany. "We went to a movie, *Cinema Paradiso,* and I cried all the way through it. That broke the tension." Still, it would be an uphill battle for the series. ABC placed it in a less desirable time slot, Saturday nights at nine P.M. Eastern Time, preceding another struggling series, *Twin Peaks.* Traditionally, viewership is lower on Saturday nights and very few programs flourish (*Golden Girls* and *Sisters* are two notable exceptions in recent years).

Unfortunately, the news regarding *China Beach*'s second life wasn't good for Ricki. Although the series would be returning in the fall, the show's producers had passed on making Ricki a regular cast member. Ricki was told that the decision wasn't a reflection on her talent. The show was changing its format and there was no longer any room for the character Ricki played.

With astronomical expenses to cover every month, including an expensive car note and payments on her seven-hundred-fifty-thousand-dollar house, Ricki suddenly found herself without a job.

"Where the Day Takes You"

After her stint on *China Beach,* Ricki kept herself busy auditioning for more film roles. It was nearly a year before she landed her next part, a featured role in *Where the Day Takes You,* a low-budget film released by New Line Cinema, the same company that released her first film, *Hairspray.*

Where the Day Takes You, which marked the directorial debut of Mark Rocco, explored the lives of several runaway teenagers who banded together, struggling to survive on Hollywood's mean streets. Ricki was cast as Brenda, an overweight, love-starved runaway who came to Hollywood hoping to become a movie star. Dermot Mulroney, Balthazar Getty, Sean Astin and Lara Flynn Boyle also had featured roles. Will Smith (*Fresh Prince of Bel-Air*), Nancy McKeon (*The Facts of Life*), Alyssa

Milano (*Who's the Boss?*) and Adam Baldwin also received billing for special appearances they made in the gritty film.

Ricki valued the chance to appear in the movie because it promised to take a realistic look at the issues and problems confronting runaway teenagers. It also gave her the chance to work with the handsome Dermot Mulroney, whose work she admired. On the down side, because *Where the Day Takes You* was a low-budget movie, it paid barely better than scale.

The cast prepared for their roles by researching the lives of real-life runaway teens. They visited centers where desperate teens turn for help, drug rehabilitation centers and Teen Hot Line offices. "I spent a lot of time at the Los Angeles Youth Network," said Ricki. "I met this girl named Adonna, who was really tough, but we bonded." Since moving to Los Angeles two years earlier, Ricki had generously contributed her time to such organizations as AIDS: Project Los Angeles, which provided services to people living with AIDS. However, nothing prepared Ricki for what she learned at the Los Angeles Youth Network about teens who are forced to live on the streets because they've either run away from home or were disowned by their families. Ricki also met teens who were like Brenda, fantasizing about a show-biz acting career. "So many of these kids come to Los Angeles thinking they're going to be stars," Ricki said.

"We learned a lot when we went and met with these kids," said Lara Flynn Boyle. "Sometimes it can be very depressing, but they're hopeful too, and they are really trying to make the best of their lives."

"I went to heroin rehabilitation centers. I went to a couple of halfway houses," revealed Sean Astin. "I went with a friend of mine and talked to kids that he knows about living on the streets, and what it's like using drugs."

Talking with teens on the streets, Ricki learned of their backgrounds and discovered that their reasons for being in the dire situation they found themselves in were complex and often tragic. "You can't possibly know what these kids go through until you're face to face, talking with those who live it day by day," she said. "And as bad as it is for them on the street, it's often hard to find fault since it's sometimes worse for them at home. It's a double-edged sword."

Director Mark Rocco was impressed with the preparation and dedication of his ensemble cast. "They put the art of acting ahead of being in teen magazines," he said. "This was important to me, and I was delighted that they completely threw themselves in it."

Ironically, several key scenes from the movie were filmed on streets that were just a few minutes' drive from Ricki's comfortable home in the Hollywood Hills. However, the piercing sound of gunshots that occasionally rang out when the cast was filming at night served as a reminder that this was a world very unfamiliar to Ricki. Hundreds of teens who lived on the streets were hired to work as extras in the movie and paid forty dollars a day. Ricki found herself charmed by some of the kids, but she also understood it was unlikely she would ever develop long-lasting friendships with them because of the unpredictability of the lives they were leading. "You've got to really hang in there," she said, thinking of what she had learned from the teens who worked as extras on *Where the Day Takes You*. "It's a tough situation for a lot of these kids: They can't even work or go to school, because you need an address and some identification to do that. They really get stuck in the middle."

The experience also left Ricki feeling grateful that her own years as a teenager had been relatively problem-free. "My interest in the arts was a huge diversion," she offered. "I rebelled a bit at nineteen by dating bad boys, but my mom always hated my boyfriends and still does."

*   *   *

Although *Where the Day Takes You* was generally
well-received by film critics, several expressed
their disappointment at the role Ricki played. *Variety* wrote, "Ricki Lake deserves better than this
minor role, in which she's the butt of fat jokes."

Even though the response by film critics was
generally favorable to Ricki's performance, the
comments in the *Variety* review as well as in other
papers all mentioned the jokes about her character's weight in the movie. Ironically, it wasn't how
the part was originally written. During the filming
of the movie, Balthazar Getty ad-libbed several derogatory comments about Brenda's weight, in the
guise of his character, and the director, to Ricki's
chagrin, decided to keep them in the movie.

By the time Ricki was finished filming *Where the
Day Takes You*, she was beginning to tire of her
weight. It even affected Ricki's attitude toward
her love life. "The guys that I'm interested in are
the guys that bug me," she said. "I get all the
chubby-chasers."

But a few other events would have to take place
in Ricki's life before she decided to do something
about her weight.

"Rock Bottom"

In the spring of 1991, Ricki's life was spiraling out of control on every front. By the time her season-long stint on *China Beach* ended, she had gained fifty pounds. "I was the heaviest at that point," she said. "When you're two hundred pounds and you gain fifty, you're huge." At her heaviest, Ricki was carrying two hundred fifty pounds on her five-foot-four frame. She wore a size twenty-four dress.

With auditions few and far between, Ricki found herself turning more and more to food to help ease her anxiety. Unfortunately, she wasn't choosing the most nutritious foods. A burger and fries were considered regular fare for lunch, followed by a rich dessert. When she was in the mood for a snack, the drive-through windows at McDonald's and Wendy's were also frequent stops for Ricki. "I ate everything that wasn't good for me," she said. "I was totally unaware of what I was doing to my body."

Ricki's actress friends, young starlets who depended on a svelte figure to guarantee future roles, often questioned Ricki about her food choices and gently suggested she consider low-fat alternatives, acting on the belief that it might help her land more work. "All my friends were skinny ingenues eating salads," recalled Ricki, "while I ordered the burger and fries, because in my mind, I was in a category all by myself."

Until Ricki hit her dry spell, she didn't see any reason to change her eating habits. If anything, she felt her weight worked to her advantage. Other than Roseanne and Delta Burke, how many other overweight actresses were as well known? "Things were absolutely going well for me. After *Hairspray* I was the new kid on the block, who was fat and a movie star. It was working for me. I was getting jobs left and right. I mean, I was as happy as can be. Because I'm fat, you know, and they're hiring me *because* I'm fat," Ricki explained. "I had that constant reinforcement that I could eat whatever I wanted because I had a career. I was a fat movie star. They didn't want me to change. I was probably insecure."

Ricki also felt that because she was comfortable with who she was, it made the people around her feel comfortable. When people met her they were always pleasantly surprised to find that she was remarkably similar to Tracy Turnblad, the charismatic, endearing character she'd played in *Hairspray*. "The character I played in *Hairspray* was really me," said Ricki.

Ricki also had another reason for feeling that her weight wasn't an issue. In addition to working regularly and being well liked, she was also never at a loss for boyfriends. Regardless of her size, she always managed to have a romantic relationship. "My weight never hurt me when it came to guys. It's true that I was older than most girls when I became sexually active—I was twenty when I first had sex—and being overweight probably had something to do with that," she said. But Ricki also maintained a healthy attitude toward sex. She enjoyed flirting and receiving attention from men. Since her arrival in Hollywood, two years earlier, she had enjoyed good relationships with men, with the exception of one, where she felt the guy's behavior toward her bordered on abusive. It was also Ricki's experience that her weight separated the men who were really interested in her from the ones who only wanted to be around because of her status as a successful movie star. If a guy pursued a relationship with Ricki, she was confident that he was going beyond the superficial and appreciated her for who she was as a person. Consequently, despite the advice of well-meaning friends, Ricki never saw a reason for trying to lose weight. "Being fat was who I was, it was just part of my personality," she said. Ricki didn't perceive losing weight as being an improvement because things had been running smoothly in her life.

But when Ricki had difficulty persuading her agents to line up auditions for her, she started to think twice about her weight and how it was affecting her life. She began to realize that food had always been her top priority. If she went to Disneyland with friends, she viewed it as an opportunity to sample the diverse variety of foods at the different booths. Food was the focus of her life. While her friends were considering what exciting ride they wanted to take next, Ricki was lagging behind, wondering where she could pick up some ice cream to tide her over until they had lunch. She derived more enjoyment from touring the candy stores at Disneyland than she did riding on Space Mountain.

After completing an acting role, Ricki arranged to keep the outfits she wore because she dreaded shopping for new clothes and avoided stores for "oversized" women like the plague. "The idea of it made me break out in hives," she said. Meanwhile, she thrilled at the idea of finding a new, cute hat to add to her collection. "They were the only thing that fit me," she explained. When Ricki visited large department stores, she bypassed the makeup counters, and rarely got her hair cut at trendy Beverly Hills salons. It was all part of her denial regarding how she really felt about herself as an overweight woman. She skillfully camouflaged her size in formless, baggy clothes that always included an elastic waist. Whenever she began work on a new movie and wardrobe asked for her measurements, Ricki would fib and offer smaller sizes. On her California driver's license, she listed her weight at one hundred sixty pounds. Who'd ever find out? she reasoned. Even if she happened to be stopped for a traffic violation, squad cars didn't come equipped with a scale to weigh her.

When Ricki reached a stage in her career where her agents weren't even bothering to return her calls, let alone drum up auditions for her, it became crystal clear that her weight was a factor. Ricki suspected that when her agents did call casting directors for an audition, they were flat out responding, "Yeah, we know Ricki. She's too heavy for the part we have in mind." "It wasn't working for me anymore. The fat thing was over. Directors were saying, 'You know, Ricki—she's not right, she's too fat,'" she said.

Even her love life was on a downslide. Although she was in a serious relationship with an actor, they bickered constantly. When Ricki fretted about why she wasn't working, he'd use the opportunity to throw her weight back in her face. If she reached for a cookie to comfort herself, he'd blow it out of proportion and say her appetite for cookies was the reason she couldn't get work.

Ricki also sensed that her weight was adversely affecting her health. Although she was still a young woman in her early twenties, Ricki preferred sedentary activities, such as reading or watching television to playing tennis or roller-skating. Eventually, she noticed that a simple walk up a single flight of stairs caused her difficulty. "It was hard to move. I'd walk up stairs and be breathing heavy," she said. Yet Ricki's phobia of seeing a doctor, and being forced to stand on a scale, prevented her from seeking medical treatment. "I would literally like shake and freak out if I had to go to the doctor," she said.

*   *   *

With the bank constantly calling, requesting the
monthly payment that was already overdue on the
mortgage, Ricki turned to her father for help. Realizing the bind his daughter was in, Ricki's dad
Barry loaned his daughter money to assist her during the bleak times. Ricki appreciated the financial
aid from her father, and made it clear she'd repay
him as soon as her luck turned around. "I couldn't
afford the payments on the house I was living in. I
was struggling for the first time in my life." With a
new payment due every month, and the prospects
looking bleaker career-wise, Ricki became more
and more aware that she might have acted prema-
turely making such an expensive, long-term pur-
chase. "It was a huge mistake. I was twenty years
old. I didn't know how hard it would be to pay a
mortgage," she said. Combined with the massive
expenses she incurred having the roof repaired,
along with the gardener hired to maintain the
premises, as well as a maid who kept the house
in order, Ricki was unable to keep up. "I didn't
understand," she explained.

Ricki's hopes were raised when she read a new
screenplay titled *Dogfight* that was scheduled to go
into production. River Phoenix was already
attached to the project in the lead role. *Dogfight*
told a tale of a young man who romanced an inse-

cure, plain waitress, hoping to win a bet he'd made
with his buddies to bring the most unappealing
girl to a party. Eventually, he fell in love with the
girl. The story was set in the sixties, and reflected
the changes that took place in that turbulent period when, among other things, crew cuts gave
way to shoulder-length hair. Ricki felt the role of
the young woman was made for her; she understood exactly how the character felt and was con-
vinced she could convey it in her performance. But
to Ricki's dismay, the director of the film felt differently, and instead cast Lili Taylor. "I lost it because I was too fat," said Ricki, who for the first
time was experiencing a direct, stinging rejection
because someone in a position of power felt she
was too heavy.

Ultimately, Ricki decided to turn the pain of losing the part in *Dogfight* to her advantage. Determined to make a change in her life, Ricki resolved
to take action by losing weight. "Things couldn't
get much worse than they already were. Everything in my life was at a standstill," she said. Her
boyfriend provided further motivation by constantly stressing how much more attractive and
successful Ricki would be if she would only do
something about her weight. Although Ricki felt
wounded by his comments, she realized he had a
point, and it helped her stay committed to losing

weight. Eventually, Ricki broke up with her boy-friend because of other problems they were also experiencing in their relationship. "We've remained friends," she said. "I know that he never intended to hurt me, only to help."

One morning, Ricki woke up, walked to her kitchen and carefully began ridding her kitchen of every scrap of food. With a large plastic garbage bag in hand, she tossed out everything in her refrigerator. She then turned to the cupboards, picking up bags of cookies, potato chips, crackers and other edible goodies, and threw them in a bag as well. Ricki was now officially on her diet. "It got to a point where nothing was going right—financially, emotionally, physically—and I felt like the only thing I could take control of was my body," she said.

Initially, Ricki didn't share her plan to lose weight with anyone. This was something she wanted to try one day at a time. As time passed, if she was able to stick to her resolve to lose weight, it would become clear to her friends without having to say anything.

Nor did she set goals—unrealistic or otherwise. "I didn't set any goals because I didn't want to fail," Ricki explained. "If you set long-range goals, you're bound to be disappointed. On my diet, I never said, 'I'll be psyched when I'm one hundred and thirty pounds.' It was more like, 'Let me get through today and then I'll deal with tomorrow.' "

Initially, Ricki often found the going rough. Since she had never seriously committed to a diet before, every hunger pang she experienced presented a challenge not to give in and eat. In the earlier stages of her diet, Ricki nibbled on only enough food that she felt would sustain her. Since she wasn't consulting a doctor for help, this occasionally led to problems that presented health risks. "I did not lose my weight in the healthiest way," she admitted. "I went through periods where I would faint from not eating enough."

Losing weight became all-consuming for Ricki, which didn't trouble her. Nothing was happening with her career or in her love life, so she had plenty of available time and attention to turn over to her diet. Still, it was a lonely, painful time for Ricki, particularly when she was invited to public Hollywood functions, where every young starlet wearing a perfect size eight felt like an indictment of her own situation. "It was hell living in L.A. during that period," said Ricki. But gradually she began to learn a valuable lesson from sticking to her diet: It's more effective trying to please yourself rather than struggling against the impossible odds of pleasing everyone else.

As time passed, Ricki became better educated
about cutting down on fat grams. She found herself drawn to magazine articles that promised tips
on healthier eating. At mealtimes, Ricki no longer
served herself heaping portions. Instead, she doled
out smaller portions and when hunger cravings
hit, she'd reach for an apple or orange. Junk food
was permanently banned from her refrigerator,
and late-night trips to McDonald's and Wendy's
became a thing of the past.

Keeping a clear mind, Ricki understood that her
extreme diet wasn't motivated out of self-loathing
or self-hate. "I just didn't like my body," she said.
"I couldn't watch myself on screen. I rarely looked
in the mirror. I'd get on a bus and think that
everyone was praying I wouldn't sit next to them."

Ricki also recalled earlier comments she'd made
to reporters, when she didn't feel weight was a
hindrance to her, either personally or professionally. "I'm a voluptuous babe, and I think the whole
issue is that it's not a handicap," she'd told *TV
Guide* in early 1989. "Weight is not as important
as people make it, and I think they should stop
having gorgeous people on TV. The Roseanne Barr
show is a good thing, and they could use somebody
like me too. Look, I'm not the chicks on *Knots
Landing* or *Falcon Crest*. But you should see the
fan mail I get from *Hairspray* alone. All these guys

are proposing marriage to me because they're chubby-chasers."

As Ricki began to notice herself shedding excess pounds, she became more conscious about the foods she ate in restaurants. Nothing passed her lips without her first giving it careful consideration. At lunch with friends she'd surprise everyone by ordering salad instead of her usual steak. She'd also request the dressing on the side. When she prepared meals at home she trained herself to cook without using oil.

Although on the first day of her diet her kitchen was completely free of food, Ricki gradually eased up. Eventually, she learned to keep fruit, water and diet soda on hand. She found they helped her stick to her diet, particularly when she was feeling vulnerable and needed the comfort of food to help her feel better.

When Ricki first placed herself on a diet, she often experienced difficulty warding off depression because she was painfully aware of how much weight she needed to lose. She didn't even allow herself the luxury of fantasizing about slipping into smaller dress sizes because the day when that would eventually happen seemed too distant and remote. Instead, she found encouragement in the compliments paid to her by friends she hadn't seen for a while. More and more, she found herself running into people who hadn't seen her in ages and were quick to offer praise on how great she looked. By November, six months into her diet, Ricki had lost fifty pounds.

In the midst of her diet, Ricki received devastating news. Her father was in the hospital, having been savagely beaten by hoods as he left his pharmacy, located in a section of Manhattan that had become increasingly more dangerous because of drug-dealing in the area. Horrified by the thought of losing her father, Ricki rushed back East to be by his side. For several weeks her father lay in a coma. At one point, doctors pronounced him dead. But seconds later, he miraculously showed signs of life, giving Ricki and her family revived hope that he'd survive his injuries. When he regained consciousness, a thankful Ricki embraced her dad and tearfully said she loved him. Looking back on the ordeal, Ricki said, "It was terrible, and it taught me family is everything."

Soon after he was released from the hospital, Barry and his wife sold their home in White Plains, New York. They divided their time between an apartment in Manhattan and a Las Vegas vacation home. Whenever possible, Ricki traveled from Los Angeles to spend time with her parents, grateful that they were still in her life.

Ricki especially appreciated that her parents were so supportive, both emotionally and financially, as she struggled to land a new acting job and get her career back on track.

With her weight loss in full swing, an optimistic Ricki sensed better days were on the horizon for her.

9

"Rising from the Ashes"

That same year, Ricki was forced to sell her three-bedroom home. Although Ricki would miss the house, she was relieved that the costly mortgage payment would no longer be hanging over her head. Earlier in the year, she'd tried cutting back on expenses, such as the gardening and pool-cleaning. "I will never ever buy anything impestuously again," she said. "Especially a property worth nearly a million dollars. That was the biggest regret of my life."

With the help of her business manager, Ricki found a quaint guest house where she was able to live with her two cats and dog. The rent was extremely reasonable for Los Angeles, six hundred dollars a month. Ricki chose not to see losing the house as a defeat. She was, instead, grateful to have a new, more affordable home where she could continue to concentrate on moving ahead with her life.

Free from the burden of having to scrape together money for her house, Ricki had more energy to focus on new activities. After losing the first fifty pounds, she joined a gym and began a daily two-hour workout program that consisted of step aerobics, the Stairmaster and the treadmill. The workout helped to increase her metabolism, making it possible to shed even more weight in a quicker amount of time. Later, she added bicycling and swimming to her workout routine. Soon after, she was jogging. At one point, she even enrolled in a hip-hop dance class.

At first, Ricki dreaded going to the gym, feeling self-conscious about her size. But as she became more familiar with the surroundings, she realized that most people working out tend to be absorbed in their own routine and had little time to notice anyone else's imperfections. Although she was a member of a gym in Los Angeles, considered to be the fitness capital of the world, she noticed that the people who went to her gym came in all shapes and sizes. There were even members who weighed more than she did. Knowing how difficult it was for her to find the strength to walk through the gym's seemingly intimidating doors the first time, Ricki admired their courage.

As Ricki started to build her endurance, she found herself looking forward to going to the gym. Her mind no longer taunted her with flimsy reasons for passing up a workout. Instead, the workout became a part of her life. The best part was that the more she went, the more she enjoyed it—and the better she felt about herself. Eventually, she fell into a routine. "I do a half hour on the Stairmaster, weight-training, and at least one-hundred sit-ups for two hours three times a week with a trainer. It's grueling, but I need that kind of discipline," she said. She started with weights as well, which helped to add muscle tone to her body.

Ricki also continued to keep a healthy outlook regarding her workout and diet. Rather than set herself up for failure by setting unrealistic standards, Ricki chose to appreciate the positive results she was gaining from her workout, such as not having to look at a double chin when she caught a glimpse of herself in a mirror. Instead, her cheekbones began to take on a refined shape, reminding Ricki of just how much she had accomplished.

But regardless of how much she had achieved, Ricki stuck by one hard rule. "I still don't weigh myself," she revealed. "My trainer does. I don't want to get into a thing where if I gain a pound it ruins my whole day."

All of the success Ricki had enjoyed in her career, and the work it took to get there, didn't compare to the difficulty she faced shedding pounds. "Losing weight was the absolute hardest thing. I'm an emotional eater—when I get upset the first thing I think about is food. Everyone asks, 'How'd you do it?' It's obvious. You've got to not eat for a long period of time and you've got to exercise," she said.

To show how much her life had changed, Ricki now enjoyed eating low-fat foods. She even gave up red meat, which had once been a staple in her daily diet. Occasionally, she'd find herself hitting a wall where, no matter how little she ate, or how much she worked out, she wasn't able to lose as much as a single pound. But Ricki is proud to boast that in the three years since she first dumped out the food in her refrigerator, she's never regained any significant amount of weight. She believes the secret to keeping the weight off is sticking to a consistent meal plan. Ricki knew too many people who had lost weight on crash diets, ate healthy for a period of time and then gradually slipped back to their former eating habits. When she absolutely craved an ice cream bar, or piece of pie, Ricki wouldn't deny herself. Instead, she'd spend more time at the gym. She was also clear that the serving of dessert was something rare and not to be continued on a regular basis.

Ricki's weight loss eventually changed her life in more ways than she had ever imagined or anticipated. She started to enjoy looking at her reflection in the mirror. If a friend suddenly shot a candid photo of her, she didn't protest. Nor did she cringe when she saw the photo. What surprised Ricki was how much she had been in denial about such things when she was overweight.

Naturally, as people became more aware of Ricki's weight loss, magazine editors asked to write features on how she had done it. Ricki gladly consented to the interviews, proud of her success. Unfortunately, she experienced a backlash from some people who were overweight and, according to them, proud of it. They felt Ricki did a disservice to other overweight people by publicly sharing details of her weight loss and how much it had changed her life. "Some people say that I've sold out, you know. I was this role model for heavy people. But the thing is, I never set out to be a role model at all, and I don't set out to be one now. I won't preach to anyone and tell them how to lose weight. I don't know any better than the next person," she said. "I'm just me. I'm going to do what I need to do, first and foremost."

Ricki also thought that by candidly discussing her weight loss in the media, she might inspire other overweight people who had doubts they could accomplish the same thing. Ricki felt if she could do it, anyone could. Before she began her diet and workout program, Ricki used to identify herself as the laziest person alive.

By the same token, she had no desire to set herself up as a diet guru who knew all the secrets; that was best left to the Susan Powters and Richard Simonses of the world. If anything, looking back on the early days of her diet, Ricki felt some of her techniques were foolhardy and cautioned that they wouldn't necessarily work for anyone else. But she was a firm believer that, if a person wanted to lose weight badly enough, it could be done.

Ricki's parents were also proud of what she had accomplished by losing weight. They enjoyed seeing their oldest daughter feeling good about herself and branching out in new areas of her life, such as working out. But they made it clear to their daughter they never faulted her for being overweight. Her mom Jill said, "Healthwise, I was concerned. Now I'm just pleased to see her happy and looking so beautiful."

Ricki's sister Jennifer, meanwhile, was surprised by some of the things she learned about her older sister in intimate conversations they shared after her weight loss. "I didn't know until after Ricki lost her weight how dissatisfied she was with herself," said Jennifer. "She seemed happy, but she wasn't always. I found out years later that she had a hat collection because they were the only things that fit her. That was sad."

Ricki's weight loss also opened up an entire new world to her—shopping. "I'm totally wrapped up in shopping," she said. "I love to shop. I love to go bikini shopping! No, I'm kidding. But I don't hate the way I look in a bathing suit."

Ricki can recall with fondness the day she found herself able to fit comfortably in a size-eleven dress. She realized that to some people a size-eleven may seem big. "But the first time I went shopping at that size, I started weeping in the dressing room because I could not believe a medium fit me," she said.

As time went on, Ricki found herself able to fit into smaller and smaller sizes. She remembered times when she went shopping with her friends during her heavier days. At the end of the day, her friends would pile into the car, loaded down with bags of new clothes. Meanwhile, Ricki would return home empty-handed because nothing fit her.

Friends who were familiar with Ricki's former eating habits also wanted to know how she found the discipline to turn down cake at the end of a meal. They still had vivid recollections of Ricki scanning the dessert menu before she had even or-

dered her meal. Ricki quietly explained to them
that she gained more pleasure from fitting into a
cute little dress bought at a place such as Betsey
Johnson than she did cramming a three-layered
hunk of chocolate cake in her mouth.

With her weight loss, Ricki began developing
new tastes in clothing styles. She ranked J. Crew's
and Tweeds' sporty, comfortable clothes at the top
of her list of favorite things to wear. Yet she still
enjoyed searching for clothing bargains.

By the time *Where the Day Takes You* was released, Ricki had already lost considerable weight.
At a screening of the movie, Ricki remembered
feeling uncomfortable seeing herself, especially
blown up on a large movie screen of epic propor-
tions. "It's hard to watch the movie because I'm
sixty pounds heavier," she said. When the cable
network Lifetime began showing reruns of *China
Beach,* Ricki caught an occasional episode. The
image that she saw flickering on her twenty-inch
television set was tangible evidence of how much
she had changed, both physically and emotionally.
"It makes me cringe. I can't believe I let myself
get to that point. It seems like a different person.
I can't even remember that period," she revealed.
In regard to her earlier work, Ricki added, "The
fact that I'm forever trapped in celluloid looking
like that is frightening."

With her dramatic weight loss altering how she looked, Ricki realized it would ultimately affect her ability to land new acting roles; consequently she had no problem being the first to point out that she had lost weight. "My being fat was a gimmick and now my being like a normal person is a gimmick," she said. "It was definitely calculated. I looked at the business and decided you have to stand out in some way to get work. It'll be nice when people don't care anymore."

Even though Ricki was quick to give herself a pat on the back for what she had accomplished, she doubted that she would ever have had a career in films had she not been overweight. "If I were to start out today, I still wouldn't be thin enough or pretty enough to break through," she insisted. "It's true, it's true."

After three years of changing the way she ate, Ricki revealed she had lost a total of one hundred twenty pounds. "I lost almost one of me," she observed with pride. "It was as much weight off my head as it was weight off my body, though. There's a whole issue with food and how people treat you and how you're discriminated against. Living my life as a fat person and then living my life as a thin person is a totally different experience. I'm really glad to be living my life as I am now. It's more fun."

In a more serious mood, Ricki discussed how she felt the first time she flipped through an old photo album. "When I look at old photos, I can't believe I loved myself, let alone anyone else loving me," she said.

On the issue of love, Ricki found herself questioning her own values, as well as the values of the potential new love interests in her life. "Shouldn't you love someone unconditionally?" she wondered. "But doesn't a person have a right not to be sexually attracted to another? It's confusing. It's something I can speak about from the heart—or gut, as they say."

After losing her weight, Ricki learned firsthand how much weight can affect a guy's interest. Occasionally, she'd run into some good-looking guy she knew from her heavier days. Usually, he'd be someone she had once been attracted to, but who had never shown any interest in her. Suddenly they all were asking for her phone number, suggesting that maybe they get together for dinner or a movie. Rather than feeling flattered, Ricki found herself holding back anger. She still remembered how they had reacted to her when she was overweight. Consequently, she definitely didn't have any interest in pursuing even a casual acquaintance with any of them.

However, there was one special guy who succeeded in capturing Ricki's heart on the heels of her weight loss. His name was Tom Booker. They met when Ricki guest-starred in, of all things, *The Real Live Brady Bunch,* a play based on old *Brady Bunch* scripts that had enjoyed a good run in Chicago and New York before arriving in Los Angeles. Booker was one of the cast members. Although Ricki found Booker very handsome, she was drawn to him because of his sharp sense of humor. Soon after Ricki's appearance in *The Real Live Brady Bunch,* she and Booker were a regular item. "I'm having the best relationship," she said. "I was in a bad one for a long time. Now I'm seeing the light." Ricki was so taken with Booker that she added, "This is the first relationship I've been in where I don't even look at another guy."

One reason Ricki enjoyed being with Booker was that they had a lot in common. On weekends, one of their favorite things to do was browse through the movie listings in the newspaper, searching out bad movies to see. They also enjoyed bowling together. Ricki, a self-professed dog lover, also appreciated that Booker had a fondness for dogs as well. "I can't imagine my life without him," she said.

Ricki's professional life was also starting to turn around. She was cast as comic Pauley Shore's college girlfriend in *Encino Man* (unfortunately, her part ended up on the cutting room floor before the film was released). Best of all, she was cast as the lead in a horror movie titled *Skinner*. Not only was it a lead role, she was playing a glamorous, beautiful character. Understandably, Ricki considered it a breakthrough role. Unlike several of the roles she had played in the last two years, she wasn't cast as the lead girl's overweight friend. What Ricki enjoyed most about reading the script was that there wasn't a single reference made to her character's weight. "It was an amazing thing to have a script that didn't mention the word 'fat' even once—finally," she said.

Skinner also introduced Ricki to something else she hadn't experienced in movies before, playing an honest-to-goodness love scene. "When you're overweight, love scenes aren't taken seriously," she noted. Despite her excitement over being cast as the leading lady, Ricki experienced trepidation about playing the love scene, partly because it involved heavy petting. "The love scene in that flick was hard for me," she said. "I wore underpants and a T-shirt. But it was kind of offensive being groped. I felt violated." Surprisingly, Ricki added, "It would have been easier if I'd been heavier." Still, Ricki was pleased with how the movie ended. "I almost get killed," she revealed, "but I don't because I'm the babe!"

*   *   *

As much as Ricki was enjoying her newfound success, both in her personal and professional life, she understood that it could all instantly fall apart again if she reverted back to her former eating habits. Ricki freely acknowledged that she considered food her drug of choice and she understood the powerful effect it continued to hold on her. "I don't take drugs. I don't drink. My downfall is food," she said. "It's a constant battle to fit into little size-ten suits."

By the fall of 1992, Ricki had lost more than a hundred and twenty pounds. "Losing all this weight is my single greatest accomplishment. I feel better and better and better," she said.

Soon after, Ricki was trying on new clothes in a store when she made a discovery that thrilled her. She fit into a size eight dress. It was only eighteen months earlier when she was embarrassed to admit she wore a size twenty-four. "I was freaking out!" she exclaimed. "I was sooo psyched."

Meanwhile, the biggest opportunity of Ricki's life was waiting just around the corner; one that would move her career into an entirely new direction.

10

"Wanted: Vibrant, Young Female to Host TV Talk Show"

In early 1992, Garth Ancier, the network programmer responsible for launching the Fox Broadcasting Network, and Gail Steinberg, an Emmy Award-winning television producer of TV talk shows, put their heads together and brainstormed about creating a new kind of TV talk show.

With Ancier and Steinberg's respective backgrounds, it was an ideal partnership. During Ancier's tenure at Fox, he and his programming team developed such hit series as *Married . . . With Children*, *21 Jump Street*, *The Tracey Ullman Show*, *The Simpsons*, *Totally Hidden Video* and *In Living Color*. Ancier also co-developed *Cops* with STF Production's Stephen Chao. Meanwhile, Steinberg had a long and outstanding association with *Donahue*, where she served as producer and senior producer for six and a half years. During her tenure, which began in 1981, she was the driving force behind a multitude of headline-making programs. In 1982, as producer, she made *Donahue* the first national television program to explore the AIDS epidemic. She followed *Donahue* with *CBS This Morning,* where she was closely involved with the program's development and subsequently played a significant role in the smooth transition when Paula Zahn joined the program as co-anchor. In April 1989, Steinberg became senior producer of *Geraldo,* where she remained until 1992. Ancier and Steinberg also had experience together creating and launching a talk show. Their first joint effort was *Jane,* a talk show which featured Jane Pratt, editor of *Sassy,* and which enjoyed a thirteen-week trial run on WNYW-TV, a Fox-owned-and-operated station. "Jane was going after teenagers," said Steinberg. But with their new show, Ancier and Steinberg's focus was on targeting young adults.

While trying to come up with a format for their new talk show, Ancier and Steinberg sampled the TV talk shows that were already in production, including the phenomenally successful *Oprah Winfrey Show; Donahue,* syndicated television's longest running talk show; *Geraldo,* which generated newspaper headlines when Geraldo Rivera broke his nose in 1988 while trying to break up a fight between a black civil rights activist and a white supremacist; *The Sally Jesse Raphael Show;* and *The Montel Williams Show,* a relative newcomer in the ever-increasing, crowded talk show arena. They quickly realized that millions of viewers were being ignored, the eighteen-to-thirty-four-year-old demographic group which was very appealing to advertisers because of its spending power. Based on their findings, Ancier and Steinberg initiated a massive search, scouring the country to find the ideal candidate who could successfully draw younger viewers to a TV talk show. "Garth and I recognized a void in the marketplace," said Steinberg. "We set out to do a show that would appeal to eighteen-to-thirty-four-year-old women who weren't watching talk shows very much. To accomplish that, we felt we had to have someone with enough life experience to have a worldview."

Word quickly spread that Ancier and Steinberg were looking for a young woman to host her own talk show. Eventually, more than a hundred hopeful journalists, actresses and models traipsed through their office, hoping for a shot to challenge the reigning queen of daytime talk shows, Oprah Winfrey. They included actresses Rae Dawn Chong and Melissa Rivers, model Veronica Webb and singer Carnie Wilson. With their heads spinning from the polite chatter they endured while talking to the would-be hosts, Ancier and Steinberg began to feel a little apprehensive. Out of the bunch, they hadn't found one woman who ultimately had the spark they were looking for to bring their proposed talk show to life.

Supervising producer Stuart Krasnow suddenly remembered an actress he'd assisted in booking during his stint as senior talent coordinator at *Late Night with David Letterman*. He recalled that she was engaging, personable, vivacious and completely down-to-earth—the exact qualities Ancier and Steinberg were looking for in a host. He told them her name was Ricki Lake, an actress who had scored success in several John Waters movies, beginning with *Hairspray*.

Ancier immediately warmed to the idea of approaching Ricki Lake. A few years earlier, he'd had a chance to meet Ricki personally when she attended a birthday party Ancier hosted at his home for a mutual friend. Ancier remembered being very impressed by Ricki's easygoing nature, charm and warmth.

Through a friend, Ancier was able to track Ricki down in Los Angeles, where he was also based. Avoiding the red tape of first talking to Ricki's talent agent or business manager, Ancier picked up the phone and personally phoned Ricki, inviting

her to meet with him to talk about a new talk show
he had in mind.

The call came at an opportune time for Ricki,
who'd just seen her hopes dashed when a role she
was promised in a TV movie suddenly vanished.
Disappointed by the loss, especially because she
was still having trouble coming up with a steady
income, Ricki had done enough business in Hollywood to know that a promise doesn't count for
much when you're trying to land work. "You're
not just desperate because the part is perfect for
you. You're desperate because you need to work.
That's happened to me countless times in my career. I've been promised this job, I've been promised that job," she said. "That's why when this job
came around I was like, 'Yeah, sure. I've heard this
before.' So I went to the meeting, and I knew it
had to be sort of important because it was on the
Fox lot in L.A. I just took it as a meeting."

In fact, Ricki was so casual about her first meeting with Ancier, and where it could lead, that she
didn't even bother calling her agent to say she was
doing it. "I didn't even think about it," she said. "I
figured it was just another waste of an afternoon."
When Ricki was escorted into Ancier's office by an
assistant, she was delighted to find four attractive
young men, including Ancier and Krasnow, waiting to talk with her. A self-professed "natural

flirt," Ricki spent a good part of the meeting asking the young executives about themselves. "I met
with these four cute guys and all I did was flirt
with them," she said. " 'Hey, what's your sign?' I
just talked to them for a couple of hours."

As the meeting drew to a close, Ancier asked if
she'd like to host their pilot. Anxious to make
some easy money so that she could pay her rent
for the month, Ricki said yes. "I did it strictly for
the five thousand dollars they paid me for the
pilot," revealed Ricki, who, based on her experiences with her ill-fated sitcom pilot three years
earlier, doubted the proposed talk show would
ever make it on the air.

"Ricki has an exuberance that none of the other
candidates had," said Ancier. "I mean, Oprah once
left a message on Ricki's answering machine, and
she brought the tape in the next day, telling everyone, 'Oprah called me!' She's such a kid."

Steinberg, meanwhile, was impressed by the
challenges Ricki had faced in her young life, such
as losing weight, and the survival skills she had
developed maneuvering her way through the un-
predictable world of show business. "Ricki views
the world with different eyes than Phil Donahue
or Maury Povich does. So she brings the perspective of a younger person. But she also has more
experience than the average twenty-five-year-old

because this is a young woman who's been out on her own in a very competitive, demanding field since she was eighteen. And I think, too, her experience growing up a heavy adolescent and young adult gave her empathy that I think many of us don't develop until we're older—if at all," Steinberg said. "Ricki is really young. She's very comfortable with being twenty-five—that's who she is. But she's also equally comfortable with having sort of an old soul."

"I really believe if I hadn't changed and gone through the things I did in the past two years, none of these other good things would be happening right now," said Ricki. Looking back on her good fortune, when she lucked out and won the lead role in *Hairspray* while still in college, Ricki realized that she'd gone through a period in her life when she considered such breaks as something that was left to the fates, as if she didn't have a hand in making it happen. "Before, I thought of my career as a game, but now I'm much more serious about it. I saw how it could all disappear," Ricki said.

When a reporter asked Ricki if she thought she would've gotten the chance to host her own talk show if she were still overweight, Ricki candidly answered, "I know they wouldn't have hired me for this job because I was way bigger than Oprah at her heaviest."

But Ricki's producers insisted that wasn't the case, especially because Krasnow had recommended Ricki based on an appearance she'd made on *Late Night with David Letterman* in the late eighties, when she was nearing two hundred pounds. Since that appearance, he hadn't been in contact with Ricki. "When we contacted Ricki, we didn't even know that she had even lost the weight," said Steinberg.

Regardless of whether or not Ricki would've been hired to host her own talk show if she was still overweight, Ricki still felt the commitment she had made to losing weight had created a profound impact on her life. "The weight change was a really big emotional growth for me. I took back control of my life and grew up," she said. "By the time I moved to New York, I was a different person."

After landing the stint to host a talk show pilot, Ricki recalled an experience she'd had several years earlier, when she was touring the country promoting *Hairspray*. The publicity blitz included a stop in Chicago, where Ricki appeared on *The Oprah Winfrey Show*. "Of course, I watched her all the time when I was young. I could relate to her because we were both heavy," said Ricki. Ricki identified with Oprah so much, in fact, that she shared a secret with the charismatic talk show host. "I told her I wanted to be the white Oprah," Ricki revealed, "but I never thought I'd have my own talk show at twenty-five."

Ricki taped a batch of trial shows, which made up the pilot, during the week of August 24, 1992, at WOR-TV's studios in Secaucus, New Jersey, close to New York City. "It was a conscious decision to do our talk show in the New York area," said Ricki. "I found that New Yorkers are so outspoken about their opinions, and that's what we need for this show, audience participation."

Topics for the sample shows included "Men Who Think They're God's Gift to Women" and one that Ricki felt a strong empathy for, "My Boyfriend Thinks I'm Too Fat!" Garth Ancier proved himself to be a man who puts his money where his mouth was by putting up seventy-five thousand dollars of his own money to help cover the costs of the pilots. Meanwhile, after a rough beginning, finding enthusiastic young people to attend the tapings wasn't a problem—even though the shows wouldn't be broadcast on television. The audience members knew Ricki from her movies, and were excited by the chance to see her in person.

Ricki essentially handled herself in the pilot tapings with enthusiasm and warmth. She gently kidded with the studio audience, and encouraged them to express their opinions regarding the topics that were being explored. Although she had been given prepared questions to ask, which were written on index cards, Ricki was quick to ask her panelists things that were also on her mind. Watching Ricki in action, Ancier and Steinberg had no doubt they'd made the right decision in offering her the hosting gig. Ancier was particularly impressed by Ricki's lack of nervousness on camera. It was as if she was hosting the show from her own living room and had invited two friends over to join her for an intimate evening of spirited conversation. "Put me on TV and I sweat and have heart palpitations. Ricki's completely natural," Ancier said.

Ancier also recalled a significant moment that best showed Ricki's relaxed attitude toward being in front of a television camera. "When we were doing the pilot, she was sitting with us, eating cookies and talking. Then she said, 'I have to do David Letterman now,'" he revealed.

That night, Ancier tuned in to *Late Night with David Letterman* to catch Ricki's appearance. After Letterman introduced Ricki, she glided onto the stage, accompanied by enthusiastic applause from the studio audience, and greeted Letterman with a warm smile. "She walked on and said, 'Hi, Dave,'" recalled Ancier, who was struck by the sheer naturalness of Ricki's greeting. "Other people on his show that day were in the hall hyperventilating, practicing how they'd say hello to Dave," he added.

In a conversation with Ancier regarding her appearance on *Letterman,* Ricki explained that she's never felt panic appearing in front of a camera. "Taking my SATs, I was nervous," said Ricki, "but I've always been comfortable in front of the camera. I can't get nervous. It's what I love to do. What could possibly go wrong? I could trip and fall? Worse things have happened to me."

Of course, when it came to Letterman, Ricki had another reason for feeling comfortable every time she appeared on his show. They shared a private, running gag. In an appearance on *The Maury Povich Show,* Ricki revealed that the first time she was a guest on Letterman's show he kissed her hand. "The next show he kissed me on the cheek, and the following show he kissed me on the lips," she said. By the time Ricki made her fourth appearance, Letterman took the joke to its natural conclusion. "He nailed me," Ricki said. "He fully kissed me. I almost passed out."

While in Chicago to promote her upcoming talk show, Ricki had the good fortune of being reunited with Oprah Winfrey. Steinberg, who knew Oprah from his days in Chicago producing *Donahue,* phoned Oprah. "I told her that Ricki would love to watch the best in action. I asked, 'Could we come watch the show like regular guests in the studio?' And Oprah said, 'Of course. What day? How soon can you get here?' She literally opened her arms to us. She took Ricki around and hugged her. And Oprah was really funny. They hadn't seen each other since Ricki had lost all that weight. During that time, Oprah had shed quite a few pounds too, and she told Ricki, 'Girl, you look fabulous; you must have lost a ton of weight.' She took us all around and she couldn't have been kinder." Steinberg added, "She was uncommonly generous to us."

During Ricki and Oprah's meeting, Oprah shared her own fondness for hosting a talk show. She told Ricki it was a rewarding experience because of the opportunity she'd have to learn fresh insights about human behavior every day. Considering Oprah's acknowledged reputation as "the best in the business," it was an invaluable opportunity for Ricki to literally learn firsthand how Oprah approaches her job. Among other things, Ricki was impressed by the pride and joy Oprah's staff took in their jobs. Ricki also admired how relaxed Oprah appeared literally seconds before she was scheduled to begin her show. At the end of the show, Ricki quietly watched as Oprah personally

greeted each and every member of the studio audience. Often, she touched her fans by the hand or
hugged them with genuine affection. Afterwards,
Ricki told Oprah how impressed she was watching
the show from behind the scenes.

"She was so generous," said Ricki about
Oprah's invitation to visit her studio. "She didn't
have to do that. There are all these talk shows—
seventeen of them out there now. She didn't have
to go out of her way like that." As Ricki and Steinberg prepared to head back to New York, Oprah
gave them hats and T-shirts bearing *The Oprah
Winfrey Show* logo as mementos of their visit. In
their last conversation, Oprah revealed that she
remembered the comment Ricki had made several
years earlier about wanting to be a "white Oprah"
and said how appropriate it was that she'd now be
hosting her own talk show. "Back then I told her
I wanted to be the white Oprah—which I meant as
a complete compliment, never thinking I would do
just that!" Ricki said.

Ricki's publicity blitz to Chicago turned out to
be an embarrassment of riches for her. Jerry
Springer, who also tapes his show in Chicago, also
invited Ricki and Steinberg to attend as guests.
When Springer announced to his studio audience
that Ricki would be unveiling her own show in the
fall, they responded with enthusiastic applause.

Back in New York, Ricki reflected on her visit with Oprah and thought about the qualities that made her the leader in her field. "Oprah is who she is. I've learned a lot watching her," said Ricki. "The highest compliment anyone could say to me is that I possess the qualities that she has."

The visit also gave Ricki ideas about what she wanted to do with her own talk show. "Like Oprah, I'll deal with a lot of relationship issues. But our show will look hipper, go faster," she said. "For example, while other talk shows have on six guests, we'll have on twelve, since we want to appeal to younger audiences."

Soon after her visit with Oprah, Ricki found herself embroiled in a controversy regarding comments attributed to her in *Self* magazine. In an article promoting her new talk show, Ricki shared plans for the program and expressed opinions about a "thin" Oprah, compared to a "heavy" Oprah, and how it impacted on Winfrey's show. "If you watch Oprah—who, don't get me wrong, is my hero—you'll notice that when she's heavier, the pace is slower," Ricki was quoted as saying. Immediately after the issue hit the stands, papers across America ran excerpts of the article in *Self* magazine, including *USA Today*.

Concerned that people would have the impression she didn't hold Oprah in high regard, Ricki contacted a reporter at *USA Today* and went on record regarding her feelings for Oprah. "I love Oprah!" Ricki told the reporter. "The fact that I would say anything derogatory about her shocks me more than anyone else. I would never bash the number-one talk-show host in America. She is my hero. A huge inspiration to me. If I'm one-tenth the success she is, I'll be very happy."

After shopping their pilot of *Ricki Lake* around to various production companies, Ancier and Steinberg finally penned a deal with Columbia TriStar Television Distribution, a company with a rich history in programming for young adults. At the time, Columbia syndicated two of the highest grossing off-network reruns, *Who's the Boss?* and *Married . . . With Children* (a series, ironically, that Ancier was instrumental in getting on the air when he was at Fox). Columbia also distributed two of network television's most popular daytime soaps, *The Young and the Restless,* the top-rated soap in daytime, and *Days of Our Lives,* NBC-TV's top-rated soap.

In April, Columbia Pictures TV Distribution announced it had given a production "go" to *Ricki,* the nationally syndicated talk show fronted by actress Ricki Lake. The show had been cleared in eighty-four markets, including twenty-five of the top thirty cities—covering over thirty percent of the United States. Columbia also projected that by the time the show premiered in late summer or early September, it would have an eighty-five-per-cent clearance, with Detroit, Houston, Cleveland, Denver and Sacramento among the added clearances.

Ricki Lake was an aggressive act on Columbia's part to create a niche in the highly profitable first-run syndication marketplace. To promote Ricki's show, Columbia turned to Steve Sohmer to come up with a plan that would create interest and awareness about her show. Sohmer was awarded a multimillion dollar budget to implement his campaign.

Columbia also revealed that *Ricki Lake* would originate from New York City and would be offered to interested stations on a cash-plus-barter basis, with three minutes being withheld for national sales. The company promised that Ricki's show would be relationship-oriented and advertiser-friendly, while seeking to attract the eighteen-to-forty-nine demographics group, skewing younger than many talk shows. "*Ricki* will use relationship topics to try to wrest young-adult viewers away from cable," said Alan Perris, a senior vice president at Columbia Pictures Television.

In the meantime, Ricki was busy talking to the media, doing her part to generate interest in her new talk show. When reporters asked why Ricki was interested in hosting a talk show, she answered, "Talk shows appeal to the natural voyeur in all of us."

Reporters were also curious to discover what Ricki's thoughts were on the current crop of talk shows seen on the airwaves. Naturally, Ricki complimented Oprah's show. But when reporters asked Ricki to name a host she didn't admire, Ricki diplomatically answered, "I don't like to name names, but I don't like the ones who are sleazy and just put people on the stage to make fun of them."

With a buzz already circulating about Ricki's new show several months before it was scheduled to premiere, reporters interested in creating ink contacted Steinberg for quotes. How could Ricki Lake possibly hope to succeed in a field that was already gutted with too many talk shows exploring the same threadbare topics? they wondered. After pointing out what would set Ricki's show apart from the pack, such as her appeal to a younger audience and a faster pace, Steinberg would politely answer, "We'll have to wait and see if Lake will hit the bull's-eye."

Meanwhile, a hopeful Ricki said, "I'm never optimistic about my work, but I feel good about this show. Anyway, having a talk show is easy. Losing a lot of weight—that's hard."

Determined to do everything possible to help her new show succeed, Ricki turned to psychotherapy to insure that she was content and secure with the person she had become in the last two years. She was used to handling pressure, but she wondered, "How comfortable will I be coping with success now that I'm a thinner person?"

With several months to go before *Ricki Lake* would premiere in September, Ricki accepted offers to appear in three films, *Inside Monkey Zetterland, Cabin Boy* and *Serial Mom,* which would be directed by her old pal John Waters.

11

"Serial Mom"

In the summer of 1992, John Waters was ready to shoot his next film, a comedy titled *Serial Mom*, which explored the lives of a supposedly average middle-class suburban family, the Stuphins. The father, Eugene, was a dentist with a successful private practice. The mother, Beverly, stayed home and happily attended to their daughter, Misty, a college student who frequented flea markets for rare collectables and who had a troubled love life, and their son Chip, a senior in high school who was preoccupied with horror films. Beverly, who was described as a combination of Donna Reed, Carol Brady and Lizzie Borden, presided over her family like a mighty lioness and would do anything to maintain blissful happiness in their lives. When Misty's boyfriend started neglecting her, he suddenly turned up dead.

"With *Serial Mom,* I set out to make something
that was just like a true crime film," said Waters.
"It's a genre that Americans are very familiar with
but which had never been parodied. I knew I could
have fun with it." Waters was inspired to write the
movie based on the proliferation of such shows as
A Current Affair, Hard Copy and *Inside Edition,*
as well as docudrama TV movies, which were satis-
fying America's insatiable appetite for sensational
crimes. "Now, as soon as you commit a crime, the
agents are there and you're on TV the next week,"
he added. "I'm trying to show the humor and the
irony in this whole phenomena. Personally, I
admit that I am a participant in the whole trend. I
watch those movies and read those books."

Although Waters was an avid follower of famous
trials—he was a spectator at the trials of Patricia
Hearst and the Manson family members, and sat
glued to his television watching the Menendez
brothers' trial on Court TV when they were
charged with murdering their parents—he didn't
use a real-life crime as the model for *Serial Mom.*
He also wisely decided to make the killer in his
movie a loving mom from a relatively affluent
background. "I wanted the killer to be a woman
because most mass murderers are not," he explained. "I wanted it to be about a pretty middle-
class woman who didn't come from a horrible

background, someone who spent all day at home listening to Barry Manilow and gossiping with the garbage man. Serial Mom only really cares about her family, she's showing a new sense of family values."

As with his earlier movies, Waters once again chose Baltimore as the base for his new production. "I'm so closely associated with this town that I think it would be bad luck for me not to shoot here," he said. "Plus, so many of the people I've worked with for many, many years are still here in Baltimore. I'd worry that people in the industry would get too used to seeing me if I lived in Los Angeles. I like the whole idea of having L.A. as the place where I go to take care of business."

Waters looked forward to working with Ricki again on their third project together, especially because of the inherent joy she brings to a movie set, where the days are often long and tedious. "I never met anybody who doesn't like her. Ricki is an incredibly sane, well-adjusted winner," Waters said. He also recognized the unique element Ricki brought to his films, which helped distance them from his earlier works, which were often derided as subversive by disapproving critics. "She brings to my films something they never had before, a basic cheerfulness," he said. "I learned a long time ago that my most insane characters need somebody to contrast with."

When Ricki lost her weight, there was speculation in the media that Waters wouldn't be interested in using her again because she no longer fit the image that skyrocketed her to fame in *Hairspray*. Waters, however, made it clear he had every intention of keeping Ricki in mind for all of his projects. "She's a major part of my life," he said. "I don't care if she weighs three hundred pounds or one hundred pounds. I've had very good luck with big girls. Ricki looks good either way."

Ricki, meanwhile, was elated to be working with Waters again. No matter how much her life had changed, or the difficulties she had experienced in her career, she always looked back fondly on her memories of appearing in Waters's movies. "I was so flattered to learn that he wrote the character with me in mind," said Lake. "He is such a pleasure to be around and just goes way beyond any other director I've worked with. He surpasses them mostly because he's what I consider to be a filmmaker. Every one of his movies are his creation—it's one man, one vision. I think it's safe to say that John Waters has created his own genre in the American cinema."

Ricki especially appreciated the character Waters had created for her in *Serial Mom*. Although

Misty was besieged with boyfriend problems, she
maintained a fun spirit and enjoyed the attention
of the opposite sex. "Misty is a total flirt and I'm
the biggest flirt I know," she said.

Ricki had extremely impressive company to work
with in Waters's new film, beginning with Kathleen Turner, who was highly regarded as one of
the most talented actresses working in Hollywood.
"I wanted Kathleen Turner because I knew she
took chances—she worked with Ken Russell—and
I knew she could be a wonderful villain and a great
comedian," explained Waters. "*Serial Mom*
needed to have a certain kind of charm, which
Kathleen understood. When she killed she never
looked like a crazy person. Instead, she looked like
she'd just got a new pair of earrings. It brought
her peace of some kind, which is scary, certainly,
but a good lawyer could have got Serial Mom off."
Based on Turner's splendid performance in the
film, Waters added that he couldn't have imagined
another actress playing the role. "Not only could
no other actress play the part as well as she, but
they wouldn't 'get it' as much as she gets it," he
said. "I think audiences love seeing Kathleen
Turner evil. And she likes being evil in comedies."
When Turner first picked up the screenplay to
read, she found herself confused by what she initially perceived as the movie's disturbing tone.

Putting the script down, she thought to herself, "What's wrong with this man?" Soon after, however, she went back to the script and gradually found herself appreciating its dark humor. "I picked it up and suddenly started acting my part as I read it," she said. Thrilled by the discoveries she was making, Turner accepted the role. "That's how I choose my scripts—if I act them while I read them," she explained.

Mink Stole, who's appeared in several of Waters's movies, credited Turner with restoring an element to the director's movies that had been missing since Divine's untimely death in 1988. "On this film there's a great deal of chemistry between the cast members," she observed. "That's largely due to Kathleen. She's tough to take your eyes off of and has quite a presence on-screen. I don't think I've worked with anyone this strong since Divine."

Ricki confessed that she was apprehensive when she first learned Turner would be appearing in *Serial Mom*. "I had heard horror stories about Kathleen," said Ricki, "but she was exactly the opposite. Absolutely professional. I've never seen anybody so focused. She wants it bad; she's really hungry for a hit. She works her butt off."

Rounding out the cast was Sam Waterson as Eugene Stuphin, Matthew Lillard as Chip Stuphin and Justin Whalen as Scotty, Misty's unfaithful boyfriend. Meanwhile, Traci Lords and Patricia Hearst were among the Waters returnees. "There's a whole group, the few, who have known him forever, and who are always here for him—called back for more torture," said Hearst. "When John called, I came."

When Waters was casting *Serial Mom,* he decided to take it in a different direction than his earlier films, and consciously set out to hire actors filmgoers wouldn't necessarily expect to see in his movies. "The tone of the supporting roles was very important," said Waters. "Usually, my casts have a certain camp value, but for this movie I wanted really fine actors who you don't associate with doing my films. I didn't want to do stunt casting. For instance, as the father, Sam Waterson is very straight, supplying reaction to Mom's crimes, but he's not a boob. He's just the kind of guy everyone wants for a dad. I wanted to use them to really offset the insanity of the situation."

Sam Waterson, meanwhile, who was highly regarded for his dramatic roles, such as the lead male character in the critically acclaimed television series *I'll Fly Away,* was thrilled at the chance to perform in a comedic film role. "I used to do a lot of comedies, mostly onstage, but history tends to repeat itself, so I have been offered mostly dramatic roles over the last few years," he said. "But Kathleen and John were very enthusiastic about me doing this film, and it's turned out to be great in a way I never suspected when I agreed to do it."

Sam also received an enthusiastic vote of approval from Ricki. "Sam Waterson is great," she said. "I actually have a big crush on Sam. He's happily married and much older, but . . ." Ricki also brought a surprising subtext to her role, one that even Waters didn't originally envision, in Misty's relationship with her dad. Spinning the character into an entirely new direction, Ricki played the part as though Misty had a secret crush on her father. "I like to think that my character, Misty, has sort of an incestuous quality about her," Ricki explained.

In the middle of shooting *Serial Mom*, Waterson was told of Ricki's crush on him. With a chuckle he said, "Well, she's a really nice girl and knows how to flatter a guy."

When *Serial Mom* premiered in New York, in April 1994, the guest list for the premiere was as eclectic as, well, a John Waters movie. Following the well-received screening, which was held at a private screening room on Fifth Avenue, the guests hustled over to the Museum of Modern Art's new restaurant, Sette MoMA, for a rousing post-premiere party. Punk rocker Iggy Pop was seen holding court with independent filmmaker Jim Jarmusch. Johnny Depp attended the party with his girlfriend, model Kate Moss. Fred Schneider, of the B-52s, was glimpsed collecting autographs from Ricki, Willem Dafoe and Sam Waterson. Timing her entrance like a classic movie star, Kathleen Turner arrived fashionably late to an enthusiastic round of applause.

Reviews of the movie were generally positive and cited Ricki's entertaining performance. The *Los Angeles Village View* wrote, "Ricki Lake is radiant in her third John Waters outing," while *Los Angeles Weekly,* thankful to see Ricki in a movie that knew how to utilize her talents, wrote, "Ricki Lake, in a welcome return to form . . ."

After completing her role in *Serial Mom,* Ricki appeared in *Inside Monkey Zetterland,* as an obsessed fan who stalked the lead character, a part-time actor and struggling screenwriter. The cast also included Sandra Bernhard, Rupert Everett and Debbie Mazar. When the film was released, *Variety* wrote, "Ricki Lake provides another strong presence as a TV fanatic."

Ricki also appeared in *Cabin Boy,* which included a cameo appearance by David Letterman.

With her film work completed for the year, Ricki turned her attention to her new talk show.

12

"*Ricki*'s Debut"

Shortly before Ricki's talk show was scheduled to premiere, she received an encouraging phone call from Oprah Winfrey wishing her good luck. Based on their visit earlier in the year, as well as Oprah's knowledge of Ricki, she instinctively sensed that the forecast for Ricki's new talk show looked very promising. "She told me she knows that my show is going to be a huge hit," said Lake. "Her mouth to God's ears."

Oprah's words of encouragement were important to Ricki, who faced an uphill battle in the talk show field. By the time Ricki's show premiered, there were a total of seventeen talk shows on the airwaves, including two other freshmen shows that were also making their debut that same month, *The Bertice Berry Show* and *The Les Brown Show*. In certain markets, a viewer could watch nothing but talk shows from sunrise to sundown. Although Ricki was entering the market with one hundred thirty stations across the country committed to airing her program, representing eighty-four-percent national coverage, she was at a distinct disadvantage compared to the Berry and Brown shows. Since their respective programs had been in development longer, they had already been signed by the more desirable VHF stations (channels two to thirteen on the dial), which tended to boast more viewers because of their stronger broadcasting signal. However, a significant number of stations carrying Ricki were on the UHF band (channels fourteen to eighty-four on the dial), which had a weaker broadcast signal. When Ricki's show was being peddled earlier that year in February at the National Association of Television Program Executives convention, where decisions were made about what syndicated shows will be picked up by stations around the country, Ricki was jokingly referred to as "Ricki Late," because of her late entry into the market. The inside word was that Ricki had waited too long to be taken seriously by station programmers as a serious contender for the upcoming fall season.

Ricki, meanwhile, who had high hopes for her new series, spent the earlier part of the year relocating

from Los Angeles to New York City. Having signed
a seven-year contract to host her program, Ricki
figured she'd be spending a significant amount of
time in New York. She focused on finding an affordable apartment in Manhattan's Greenwich
Village, a downtown neighborhood which boasted
a diverse population of people from a variety of
ethnic backgrounds and income levels. Ricki, however, was drawn to the area because one of her
closest friends, John Waters, had an apartment in
the vicinity. "I moved to this neighborhood because John lives here and he said it was the best
place to live," she explained. Having visited John's
New York apartment frequently whenever she was
in town, Ricki recognized the neighborhood's appeal. In fact, by the time she was ready to move to
New York, Ricki was so familiar with the area
where Waters lived that she narrowed her own
search for an apartment down to a three-block ra-
dius.

Eventually, Ricki found what she considered an
ideal place to live, an L-shaped studio apartment
located on the fourth floor of a modern building.
Before moving in, Ricki specially ordered wall-to-
wall ivory carpeting. Since she was busy preparing
for her new talk show, she had little time available
for furniture shopping. Instead, a practical Ricki
borrowed ideas from friends, including her new ex-

ecutive producer, Garth Ancier. When Ricki visited Ancier's home in Los Angeles she admired an
oversized green-and-ivory-plaid linen sofa, as well
as a beige linen armchair. After asking Ancier
where he'd purchased the pieces, she contacted a
Los Angeles store called Corsican and special-or-
dered the sofa and armchair, and made arrangements for them to be delivered to her new
apartment in New York. "I didn't have time to
shop," said Ricki, "so I just copied him."

The one piece of furniture she brought with her
from Los Angeles was her two-thousand-dollar
king-sized bed, which had a top-of-the-line Simmons Beautyrest mattress, and was fitted with
Charisma-brand all-cotton, three-hundred-ten-
thread-count sheets. "Even when I didn't have
any money, I spent it on my bed," said Ricki. "I
call it my spider's web. Everyone who spends the
night in my bed, whether it's my mother, my sister
or a man, never wants to leave."

Sticking to her resolve not to gain weight, Ricki
continued to follow the eating patterns she had
implemented in Los Angeles. Consequently, her
New York kitchen was stocked with the same sta-
ples she enjoyed in Los Angeles, Diet Jell-O and
Diet Pepsi. "I eat most of my meals at the studio,
so there's really no need to have food in the apartment," said Ricki.

Once she was settled into her new apartment, Ricki quickly found herself feeling comfortable. "I love my apartment," she said. "It's quiet, has great sun and a great view."

Ricki was also relieved to be out of Los Angeles. During her three-year stay, Ricki watched as the city was hit by multiple disasters of epic proportion, including riots, fires and earthquakes. "This is, like, the best time to be in New York," she said.

The one thing that didn't make the move from Los Angeles to New York was Ricki's romance with actor Tom Booker. They drifted apart and eventually decided to end their relationship. As with most of her past boyfriends, however, Ricki remained good friends with Booker.

A month before Ricki's show premiered, anticipation for it was already building—at least via computer! Ancier established a computer bulletin board on the America On-Line service and invited subscribers to offer their feedback, as well as ideas on topics they'd like to see explored on *Ricki Lake*. In August, several weeks before Ricki's debut date, Ancier said, "It's fairly active already and we're not even on the air yet. People are giving us suggestions for the show." To assure that the suggestions wouldn't be read by producers from other talk shows such as *Donahue, Geraldo* and *Montel*

Williams, Ancier shrewdly arranged for the suggestions to be sent to a private mailbox.

On Monday, September 13th, Ricki launched her show with a compelling topic, "I'm Getting Married, but I Haven't Met My Husband Yet." The program featured several women who believed, through the power of positive romantic thinking, that they'd meet the guy who would eventually become their husband. In fact, they were so confident that they'd find Mr. Right that they'd even set a wedding date. They also made it clear they weren't investing time dating guys who weren't husband material.

During the show, Ricki was in rare form, asking interesting questions and listening attentively as her guests answered. She glided through the studio audience effortlessly and good-naturedly fielded opinions from her audience members. Several months after the show premiered, Ricki still considered it among one of her favorites. Recalling the program, Ricki said, "We had this girl who said, 'Hi, my name is Jennifer. I'm getting married in December 1994.' This girl plans to actively search for a husband now like it was a full-time job. I'm not kidding." The following day's show was "I Love to Steal Other Women's Men."

After Ricki's premiere show was broadcast, she waited to see how the critics responded. With sixteen other talk shows they could use to contrast with Ricki's, the young host admitted she was apprehensive waiting to read the reviews. Ricki quickly discovered she had no reason for alarm. "I don't think we got a bad review. I was kind of nervous thinking, 'Oh, no, another talk show—they [the critics] are going to kill us.' But really, the public and the people who watch us every day seem to like what we're doing, and I couldn't ask for more." Ricki also received periodic long-distance phone calls from Oprah, praising her new role as a talk show host.

As Ricki's show began to develop a rhythm, she made a wish list that contained the names of the two guests she'd most like to have on her program. They were diet and fitness expert Richard Simmons and President Clinton's daughter, Chelsea. "Richard Simmons makes me cry!" said Ricki. "I know a lot of people think he's phony, but he's not. He really cares." Meanwhile, Ricki envisioned the type of segment she'd like to see with Chelsea as a guest. "I'd surprise her by bringing on her best friend. We'd find out what it's really like to be her." She then added, "We have the perfect arena for her to come and tell about what her life is like. After all, I'm the host who's the closest to her [in age]."

*   *   *

By November, Ricki received news that made her heart soar. She had succeeded in dramatically increasing the number of women between the ages of eighteen and thirty-four who were watching her show during the daytime. In New York alone, her ratings had jumped ten percent since the show's premiere in September. Meanwhile, Bertice Berry and Les Brown were experiencing difficulty attracting viewers to their respective programs. Ricki's success confirmed that Ancier and Steinberg were on to something when they decided to create a show that would attract new viewers. "Our show is a clear voice for young people who like talk TV but can't relate to what else is out there," said Ricki. "I want to do for daytime what Arsenio Hall did for late night. I want to bring the talk show down a few degrees with hipper music and more energy."

Ricki's show moved at a very fast pace, distinctly setting it apart from the other daytime talk shows. A new crop of guests was introduced in every segment, insuring that viewer interest would continue to build during the hour. Ricki's set also had a look different from the other talk shows. There were several different doors designed for surprise entrances. Her chic, yet comfortable, set was designed by *Saturday Night Live*'s production designer, Eugene Levy, who created the set to resemble a New York loft that was cozy and hip. Throughout the show, lively music was heard. The members of Ricki's studio audience also looked different from anything that had been previously seen on a daytime talk show. They were ethnically diverse and primarily in their twenties. At the beginning of each segment, Ricki's show included a "Letterman-influenced" cut to man-on-the-street interviews that mirrored the day's topic. "I think every talk show that comes out says, 'We're different.' But clearly, from every aspect, from my being the youngest host ever, and the music and the set and the bumpers [the panels that go up on the screen before commercials] and the man-on-the-street interviews, and the surprise guests and the quizzes—from every aspect, we're completely different and we do stuff that's unexpected," Ricki noted.

Although the emphasis on Ricki's show leaned heavily on relationship-type topics, there was still room for a diverse and fun mix of programs. For her Valentine's Day program, Ricki arranged a surprise for her sister Jennifer. She invited Jennifer, who still lived in L.A., to travel to New York and appear on the show as a guest. Ricki told her sister the topic was "Sisters Who Couldn't Get Along." But it was really just a ploy to get Jennifer

on the show. Once Ricki introduced her younger
sister, she revealed the real reason for Jennifer's
appearance. Ricki surprised Jennifer on camera
with a Valentine's Day blind date. The young man,
whom Ricki had personally picked and considered
a "babe," greeted Jennifer with roses in hand.

On another show, Ricki arranged a similar scenario for members of her staff that were single.
Without their knowledge, she set them up with
blind dates. "Behind the cameras, you could see
them freaking out, going, 'Oh, my God!'" said
Ricki. Several months after the show aired, Ricki
was delighted to see that several serious romances
had developed. "A lot of them wound up going out
with these people for a long time. So that was
really a lot of fun," she said.

Ricki's program also added new wrinkles to daytime talk shows that borrowed from such tried-
and-true formats as *People's Court* and *The Dating
Game*. In one program, Ricki opened a "relationship court," where a young husband accused his
wife of being a nag. To the husband's surprise, the
judge sided with the wife and sentenced him to
learn how to be friends with her. In one *Dating
Game*-style show, mothers interviewed prospec-
tive dates for their sons. In another show, where
three men thought they were "God's gift to
women," Ricki introduced a beautiful New York

model and directed the guys to try to woo her with their supposedly irresistible charms. On another show, Ricki encouraged women in the studio audience to bid on a date with several eligible bachelors who were featured onstage. "We basically auctioned off men for dates, for charity," said Ricki, "and women in the audience went bananas. Those kinds of shows just aren't done."

Conflict also played a key role in several installments during the first season of Ricki's shows. Often, Ricki would surprise the guests by suddenly introducing people they weren't expecting, or mentioning information that they didn't realize Ricki knew. The audience loved seeing the guests caught completely off guard. Meanwhile, Ricki's producers stressed that it was all done in good fun and that the guests were told beforehand to expect a surprise. In addition, the show provided a therapist for emotionally drained guests who felt they needed a trained expert to talk with after their appearance. "We never say to someone that they are coming to be reunited with their best friend from summer camp, and then surprise them with their girlfriend saying she's having an affair with his brother," Steinberg said. "We never want to take advantage of people. We don't want to ruin people's lives, and a lot of times people thank us because they find that it really helped."

"Our show is fun. It's not exploitative. It's not crude. It's not freaks," stressed Ricki. "We're offering a clearer alternative to people who want to watch talk shows but feel they can't relate to shows on menopause or whatever—the older-skewing issues."

Ricki also said topics on her show were created with the younger viewer in mind. "We turn subjects around," she explained. "If the topic is 'My Daughter Dresses like a Tramp,' we'll do 'My Mom Thinks I Dress like a Tramp.'"

"There's a big difference between Sally [Jesse Raphael] and Ricki doing a topic," Steinberg pointed out. "Sally is, I would say, a fifty-something mother of something like seven children. Ricki is twenty-five . . . [with] no children, she's the daughter."

"What we're dealing with primarily is a lifestyle difference," said Ancier. "It's a less married population, more socially tolerant group, but one that is intellectually interested in issues that don't directly affect them. They are interested in things that do affect them like gun violence or racism, but not really international or national issues that don't relate to their daily lives.

"Look," Ancier added, "our audience is more interested in dating than marriage. They like issues about teenage pregnancy and sexually transmitted diseases, topics that affect people their age."

*   *   *

During Ricki's first season the topics that weren't relationship-oriented still reflected the emphasis on what would attract younger viewers. They included shows on shoplifting, using condoms, violence, drugs and teen pregnancy.

Ricki's first season also included explosive surprises from her energetic guests. In one installment, a pregnant young woman told her boyfriend that the baby wasn't his. In another episode, a man told his girlfriend that if she didn't lose weight she was history in his life.

Emotions often ran high on Ricki's set—especially if the situation involved sticky romantic triangles. In one show, Tasha, a married woman, complained that her husband Ed's ex-girlfriend, Becky, was creating problems for their marriage because she refused to drop out of the picture. Seconds later, Becky strolled on stage, accompanied by jeers and hisses from the audience. When Becky accused both Tasha and Ed of lying, Tasha jumped to her feet and lunged toward her adversary. As the two women stood nose to nose, shouting for each other to shut up and hurling obscenities (that were deleted for the home-viewing audience), Ricki raced to the stage and attempted to calm things down. "Excuse me, excuse me," she said. "We don't say shut up to anyone. This is an open arena. We will all be heard, we won't use bad language, O.K.?"

It was raw, unbridled emotion coming from real people. "The conflicts of real people are what people want to watch," observed Ricki. "They don't want to see a freak show. They don't want to see transsexual midgets. They want to see real people, and it's like getting a peek into the neighbor's backyard."

Unlike most of the other daytime shows, which regularly offered sordid tales of incest, loopy transvestites and guests who claimed Elvis was secretly living in their home, Ricki preferred guests who had problems her audience could identify with. Although emotions sometimes ran high, Ricki was thankful that none of her more hot-tempered guests had actually gotten physical while on the show. "I'm different from Geraldo because there has been no brawling. At least not so far, thank goodness," she said.

When a reporter asked Ricki to explain the appeal of talk shows, she answered, "I don't know where the appeal comes from exactly. But I do know from my own experience as a talk-show junkie that I was always attracted to their honesty. There are so many different genres of television that exist today: talk shows, quiz shows, and sitcoms. In the seventies and early eighties—when I was growing up, daytime soap operas were so popular because you could lose yourself in someone else's life. It was the fact that you could identify with someone else's problems. Of course, the great thing was that it wasn't your life. In a more real way, I think that's why talk shows are so popular today. These shows let people know that whatever they are going through, they are not alone. And now, there's a talk show for everyone."

Ricki also felt her show was the perfect remedy for someone suffering from the blues. "Watching people on our show can make you feel lucky," she reasoned. "If you're feeling down in the dumps, turn on a talk show and you'll feel better instantly."

Based on her full schedule, Ricki had little time to watch the competition. However, she was familiar with some of the more negative shows hitting the airwaves. "I am not a fan of Rush Limbaugh's, and I don't listen to Howard Stern, but I think there is kind of a hate element to their shows," she offered. "I would also imagine that a lot of the people who listen to or watch Stern and Limbaugh shared their opinions long before they tuned in. My show doesn't preach to people or tell them how to live their lives or what's right or wrong. I don't think talk shows really have the power, or should have the power, to do that. And it's not like *Ricki Lake* is curing cancer or finding a cure for AIDS either; what we're basically doing is offering a stage or an area where people can talk about what interests them and what bothers them and where they can be heard and have a little fun."

A sampling of topics from Ricki's show include: "Get Real, Honey, Your Boyfriend Is a Dog," "Pack Your Bags or You'll Wish You Were Dead," "I Want to Tell My Cheating Boyfriend It's Now or Never," "You're the Rudest Thing Alive . . . and I'm Sick of Your Attitude," "Mom, When My Boyfriend Gets Out of Jail, I'm Taking Him Back," "He/She Says He/She Is Bisexual but I Don't Buy It," "I Have the Hots For a Coworker and I'm Going to Tell Him," "I Can't Live Down My Bad Reputation" and "The Search for America's Sexiest Twins."

In the course of the show, Ricki constantly found herself amazed by some of the intimate details guests were willing to reveal about their lives on national television. "I'm stunned when some guy blurts out that he's cheated on his wife thirty-seven times and she's sitting right there," she said. "But I think most people come because they want to be famous for fifteen minutes, and what better way to get people in their small hometown talking about them than to come on TV?

"A lot of these people don't have anyone else, or don't feel they have anyone else, to tell their problems to. Or they want to warn others how not to make the same mistakes," she also pointed out. "In that way, the show opens doors for people."

Determined to make the most of the good fortune she was experiencing, Ricki went into psychotherapy to help her enjoy her success, as well as cope with lingering issues in her that she hadn't yet confronted. Often, in her therapy sessions, the subject of her talk show would come up. "I was talking to my therapist the other day about what I do," said Ricki. "She doesn't watch talk shows, and she had no idea what my job was like. So I brought a tape of one of my shows, and we watched it. We came to this realization that, basically, I do what she does! I facilitate communication, help bring people together, and bring them to some kind of agreement or resolution. It's wild. I would never have thought about it that way. Particularly since I do the show in front of millions of people. And I'm not a doctor. I didn't have to make it through medical school."

As Ricki's ratings continued to soar during her first season, reporters frequently asked Ricki to explain her own success as a talk show host. "They say it's the likability factor," responded Ricki. "They say I'm empathetic. I'm relatable, I'm not off-putting, I'm the girl next door."

Ricki added, "I never had a miserable life, but I've had my own small battles to overcome. All these shows are personality-driven and you have to have *something* that the audience can relate to. If not, why would they tune in? I used to watch *The Oprah Winfrey Show* religiously. I related to her, I felt she was just like me. I was overweight for so long and I know what it's like to be made fun of and feel bad about myself."

Ricki also offered, "I'm not trying to be something I'm not. I guess they feel they know me and that they can confide in me."

Regardless of the reasons for her success, Ricki was thrilled that she had found her niche. "It's perfect for me because I love talking more than anything else," she said. Ricki also remained in close contact with her parents. "I feel like a kid so much of the time. I don't want to grow up. I cut my hand really bad the other day and had to call my mom for sympathy pains."

Watching tapes of the program at home, Ricki felt excited by the progress she was making. "I think it's going great," she said. "It's like acting in a way but it's also even more gratifying. I get to have an opinion and express it during a whole hour on television—that, I think, for a young woman like myself, is very rare, and I'm very lucky."

Even though Ricki had enjoyed success starring in several motion pictures, and appeared on *China Beach* for one season, she felt a new audience was discovering her. "There are a lot of people who are watching the show who never saw my movies," she said, "and if they did see *China Beach,* they're not putting two and two together."

When topics were explored on the show that Ricki felt a particular empathy for, such as weight loss or being single, she was quick to share her own experiences with her audience. "It goes with the territory," she said. Before the show premiered, she felt apprehensive over the possibility of sharing personal details of her own life, but as she grew more comfortable in her new role, the fear disappeared. "My biggest fear is that I'll get the weight back," she revealed. "But because I am out there and it is me and it is *Ricki Lake*, I have a responsibility to viewers to be honest."

In the beginning, Ricki was surprised by the letters she received from fans discussing her weight. "For me, it's such a weird thing, because my weight loss is such a personal thing," she said. "The fact that it's turned into a 'giant success story' and I'm a role model and an inspiration to people—I never set out to do that. The show came after my weight loss, pretty much."

On her show, Ricki frequently had a chance to let her sense of humor shine. In an installment titled "Man Stealers," women who'd had their men stolen by another woman began bickering with women who were identified as "man stealers." Interjecting herself into the lively debate, Ricki said, "Excuse me, everybody. We're sitting here blaming other women and the men are just as guilty." Ricki's astute and funny observation received a round of applause from her audience, who were clearly in support of what she said.

"Personally, I had fun with the 'man stealers.' It was me, the studio audience and all these vixens. Of course, I had to stay impartial, but it was really tough," she said. "There comes a point when I have to play 'devil's advocate.' But you can't be a hypocrite either. Or off-putting."

Soon after her show premiered, Ricki was surprised to discover that her friend John Waters was a regular viewer. "He really likes my show, which blows my mind because he does not watch television. He's hoping I bring in the black audience to *Serial Mom*. I have this huge black following—I love being a homegirl. Anyway, I think it's surreal for him," said Lake, who arranged for Waters to appear on the show when *Serial Mom* premiered on movie screens the following April. "Television just makes him crazy. It makes him insane. But he's been watching me. He said he's in shock. His jaw is just open. He can't believe that I'm doing a talk show. A lot of it for him is that he discovered me. He's really proud of me and proud of himself in a way."

Speaking of Ricki's success, Waters said, "Around that age, a lot of Hollywood kids turn into jerks, acting like they are better than everyone else. Ricki doesn't ever think that, and she has a great sense of humor."

By February of Ricki's first season, *The Les Brown Show,* which had been expected to be a big hit, was already canceled. Meanwhile, Bertice Berry's show was struggling to find an audience, and Ricki's was considered the fastest-rising talk show ever. Ricki premiered with a one-point-nine rating in September. By November, she enjoyed a ten percent increase in viewers in New York alone. By late January, Ricki had more than doubled her ratings to four-point-zero (a rating point represents nine hundred forty-two thousand TV households).

Naturally, reports started to spread that Ricki

was becoming a serious challenger to Oprah's top-ranking throne. Remaining low-key about her success and the comparisons being made to Oprah, Ricki said, "I'm not Oprah. I haven't been through a lot of what she's been through, but I'm getting better at listening, storytelling. And we are completely different from anything around." She also added, "There's no way I could ever be her competition. I just want to be in the game."

On a return trip from Chicago, where she promoted her show, Ricki was proud that she was able to resist a specialty the Windy City is nationally known for, deep-dish pizza. "I'm so proud. I came to Chicago to do some show promos and I didn't even eat deep-dish pizza!" she exclaimed. "If I ate one bite of pizza, I'd gain, like, three pounds!"

Ricki's first season ended with news that confirmed she had arrived as a talented talk show host in her own right. *Ricki Lake* received three Emmy nominations, including best talk show and best host. At the Daytime Emmy Awards ceremony, Oprah Winfrey ended up being named best talk show host. As expected, Ricki was happy for Oprah's win. She was also proud to be nominated in the same category as Oprah.

"I am so much happier now, so much more comfortable with my body. I like what I look like. And for the first time in my career, I can actually watch the work that I do on this show."

One significant reason for Ricki's happiness occurred shortly after her series premiered. When she was least expecting it, Ricki fell madly in love.

13

"Love at First Sight"

With her show off the ground, Ricki had more time to spend on her personal life. In October, she was invited to a Halloween party that was also a wedding reception for a pal who had just gotten married. Ricki went to the party, but she chose not to wear a costume. It turned out to be a very wise decision. While talking to a friend, Ricki happened to look across the room and made eye contact with a handsome, dark stranger, who smiled back at her. Suddenly, it was as if time stopped. "I was talking to a friend of mine, I looked up, and I was basically like, 'Wow!'" recalled Ricki.

As her friend continued to talk, Ricki found herself mesmerized, not hearing a single word her chatty companion was saying. With her heart racing, Ricki attempted to get back into the flow of the conversation. But every few seconds, she found

166

herself compelled to involuntarily glance back at the handsome stranger. Whenever their eyes met, she'd smile pleasantly. When her friend looked in the stranger's direction, Ricki commented that she thought he was very attractive. Her friend suggested that Ricki introduce herself to him, but she decided it would be more magical if he walked across the room and approached her. It was a decidedly different course of action for Ricki, who considered flirting one of her favorite pastimes.

As the minutes passed, Ricki tossed her hair back and ran her finger across the rim of the glass she was holding, all the while glancing back at the young man who was able to command her attention from across the room. Finally, after what seemed like an eternity, he came up and introduced himself to Ricki. "We both heard trumpets," said Ricki.

After exchanging brief introductions, Ricki realized the young man, who identified himself as Rob Sussman, didn't have any idea she was a celebrity, which happily intrigued her. "It made it even cooler," Ricki said. "He's an artist, not an actor. I always wanted to date someone who had other interests besides how his auditions went." Ricki also felt a kinship with Rob because he wasn't wearing a costume either. Nor, it turned out, did he arrive with a date—another comfortable detail they shared in common.

With the loud music and noisy party-revelers, Ricki and Rob found it difficult trying to have a conversation. When Rob asked if Ricki had eaten yet, she answered no. "Would you like to go somewhere and have something to eat now?" he asked. Excited by the prospect of talking with Rob in a quieter, more sedate setting, Ricki answered yes. Within minutes, they both had their coats and were out the door.

Ricki and Rob soon found themselves at a cozy restaurant where they had an extremely romantic dinner. Their conversation raced from topic to topic. Each new piece of information introduced into the discussion, such as a favorite childhood memory, inspired another fresh thought that spun things in a compelling and new direction. Ricki learned more about Rob's work, providing illustrations for such publications as *Lies of Our Times* and *Court Action Quarterly*, and that he had a part-time bartending job. As the evening stretched into the wee hours, Ricki excused herself momentarily and headed directly to a pay phone. Before leaving the party, Ricki had promised to phone her friend and offer an update on how things had progressed. When her friend answered the phone, Ricki exclaimed, "I met the guy I'm gonna marry!"

Naturally, her friend, groggy from sleep, was

taken by surprise. "How do you know?" she asked. "You haven't even kissed him yet!"

Although Ricki couldn't offer a logical explanation for what had transpired between her and Rob, she instinctively understood that they were meant to be together. "It was love at first sight, big time," said Lake. Ironically, until that night, the idea of falling in love with someone at first sight was a concept Ricki doubted actually happened to real people; it was a fantasy that only occurred in the movies.

With the restaurant ready to close its doors, Ricki and Rob, who were reluctant to call it a night, decided to move things elsewhere. "We were naked two hours later," Ricki revealed on *The Late Show with David Letterman*. Acknowledging that things between them had moved at a breakneck speed, Ricki said, "We fell in love that *night*." Three days later they first broached the subject of marriage, and "two weeks after that he moved in."

Things continued to move quickly as Ricki and Rob continued getting to know each other. Soon after, Ricki was thrilled when Rob asked a very surprising and unexpected question. "On the night before Thanksgiving, I dropped to one knee and officially asked her to marry me," he revealed.

Ricki looked into Rob's eyes and answered yes.

"We didn't have cold feet," said Ricki, speaking of the commitment they made to their relationship. With a nod to Oprah Winfrey's highly publicized, long-standing romance with Stedman Graham, she added, "Rob's definitely not my Stedman."

Not long after, Ricki teased Rob, asking if he remembered where he was in the room when he proposed marriage. "Don't you remember you were over there, near the bed?" Lake asked.

"Was it over there?" Rob responded, remembering the event differently. "I thought I was in the bathroom."

The following March, Ricki and Rob flew to Las Vegas, where Ricki's parents now lived part-time, and married. It was a quick ceremony at the Little White Chapel with seven guests present, including both sets of parents. Ricki wore a full-length traditional white chiffon dress and white picture-frame hat. Rob was dressed in a dark suit. Despite the off-beat Vegas surroundings, and music that included "Hawaiian Wedding Song," Ricki and Rob had an old-fashioned double-ring ceremony.

"It certainly was tacky," Ricki said. "This woman minister who married us was really creepy. I was crying the whole time because I was so surprised I was getting married. I always thought I'd be an old spinster." She revealed their haste to marry was prompted by their respective parents. "There was a lot of pressure from both families to get married."

Ricki had also been concerned about the media, particularly the tabloids, which were keeping constant watch on her personal life, trying to find out if she had set a date. Envisioning helicopters flying over the church during the ceremony, Ricki figured not spending a great deal of time planning the wedding would probably minimize outside attention. Right before Ricki married, two other young Hollywood actresses, Drew Barrymore and Shannen Doherty, also wed suddenly, and received intense coverage in the media. "We're not about getting attention," said Ricki. "This is just the way it happened. It's so powerful. It just made sense." Looking back on the ceremony, Ricki added, "We both have some regrets. We're talking about doing another one at a later date."

It wasn't until May, when Ricki's talk show wasn't in production, that they were able to take their honeymoon, a two-week tour of Italy.

A year after their marriage Ricki and Rob continued to respond affectionately toward one another, as if they had just fallen in love. "We're still gooey in public," said Ricki.

Their frequent public displays of affection sometimes inspired embarrassed reactions from Ricki's mom. "I think it's too much, if you want to know the truth," she said. "But when I say something, she says, 'But Mom, we're in love.'"

"I'm closer to him than anyone else," said Ricki. "This is an issue with my mother because she feels I've replaced her, but that's a part of growing up. Rob's the primary person in my life right now. I just wish there was a more powerful word than love for what I feel."

When a reporter interviewed Ricki and Rob about their romance, they were presented with a hypothetical question. The night they met, would Rob have been interested in Ricki if she were still overweight? Looking at Ricki, Rob answered, "I don't know. I mean, if you gained sixty pounds, I would still love to roll around with you every day."

"But if you met me at two hundred and fifty pounds, you might not have approached me," Ricki responded. "That doesn't hurt my feelings, though. If you were two hundred and fifty pounds, I don't know that I would've been attracted to you either."

Shortly after their marriage, Ricki found herself still adjusting to all of the whirlwind changes that had taken place in her life during the last year. "I never thought I would be this happy this early in my life. A year ago, to know that my show would be a hit, that I'd be married and that I'd be living in New York—all these things have taken me by surprise."

Meanwhile, Rob had separate issues to confront. "Rob isn't used to the visibility stuff," explained Ricki. "And sometimes he gets a little, 'You're mine, I don't want to share you with other people.' But we deal with it. People just want to say, 'I like your show, it's nice to meet you.' It goes with the territory."

When they're not working, Ricki and Rob enjoy spending as much time together as possible. On weekends they attended an art history class together. Ricki also planned a celebration for Rob when his work was featured at the opening of a new SoHo gallery, Soup.

Soon after Ricki and Rob's marriage, they moved out of her studio apartment in the Village for a one-bedroom, rent-stabilized apartment in a lower Manhattan high-rise. When Rob moved in with Ricki, they encountered few conflicts combining their personal living habits. "We're both Virgos, so we have to be clean," Ricki pointed out. "We're pretty similar as far as keeping the house neat and putting new toilet paper on the roll when it runs out." Rob also got along well with Ricki's dog and two cats. She viewed it as a good sign that they'd make great parents—but having children was something they were putting off for the distant future. "Presently, the talk show is my priority, and I'm damn lucky to have it," Ricki noted.

The main difficulty Ricki and Rob found themselves coping with was the difference in the amount of money that they earned. "Our biggest issue is money," said Ricki. "It's weird. My financial situation is so abnormal for someone who's twenty-five, and for Rob, being a struggling artist, it's hard for him to compete with that. So we have to keep our heads straight and be secure with ourselves."

"I'm sort of coming to terms with it," said Rob. "For a while, I was cranky about it, but this is going to be the deal from now on. I have to figure out a strategy for remaining sane. She could support me, but that just seems really unhealthy and emasculating."

That September, the newlyweds sought help in credit therapy for couples to help them sort out their feelings about the financial discrepancy in their relationship. Rob expressed his discomfort at constantly watching as Ricki paid for their meals out with her credit card. "We're working on getting him a credit card so he can pay for dinner every now and then," Ricki revealed.

"Whipping out a credit card occasionally might

make things more comfortable, but I have a pretty poor credit rating at this point," offered Rob. "I'm comfortably resigned to this financial imbalance between us because as long as I'm working really hard too, we're a team. I don't want to become 'Mr. Ricki Lake.' The scale may be different, but I feel as passionate about sitting at a drafting table and drawing as she does about her job."

On the one-year anniversary of the first night they met, Ricki and Rob put on the same clothes they wore to the Halloween party and dined at the same restaurant. During the evening, they expressed the love they felt for each other by being gooey in public and kissing.

14

"Second Season"

Following its first season, *Ricki Lake* went on hiatus in May. Ricki spent the summer with Rob, blissfully happy that she was able to give her marriage her full attention, without the worries of trying to land an acting job. "It's hard to think about work sometimes when you're in love," she said. "You just want to be with that person."

Ricki also utilized the summer to take care of some personal business. She finished paying back her parents for the generous loans they had advanced her when she was having a hard time making ends meet. To show her gratitude and appreciation, Ricki added an extra ten thousand dollars as a way of saying thank you.

That same summer, while Ricki's program was in reruns, it scored the highest ratings of all the daytime talk shows in New York City. Repeats of

Ricki Lake, which aired at noon on WOR, won the time period by a wide margin, outdistancing the nearest competitor by approximately three full ratings points (each rating point represented sixty-seven thousand homes in the metropolitan New York area). The jump in New York was mirrored in cities across America. Young adults, who spent the year in school, were free for the summer and discovering Ricki in a big way.

"I'm the happiest girl," said Ricki. "I have that beautiful man of mine to go home to. My family is healthy. I have a great job that I can bring my dog to. This is a great time in my life. I've had awfully good karma the last few years."

By the time Ricki returned for a second season in September, forty-two additional stations had signed on, bringing her total to one hundred seventy stations, with a ninety-five-percent clearance across the country. In markets where *Ricki Lake* was airing in undesirable time slots, such as late, late night, when fewer people are watching television, Ricki's program was upgraded to early-fringe periods, just before the dinner hour, when teenagers were home from school and usually finished with their extracurricular activities. "We were going into daytime periods where, historically, independents had not programmed talk shows," said

Ed Wilson, Columbia TriStar senior vice president of syndication. "You know, affiliates who are losing audience to a talk show, so not only would they like to buy us to shore up their early fringe, but they want to buy us to get away from their early news," he added.

In some markets, such as San Francisco, Ricki was moved to slots directly opposite *The Oprah Winfrey Show*. "We're establishing a whole new following and bringing in new viewers. The fact that we're number two to *Oprah* simply means that we have a lot of eighteen-to-forty-nine viewers watching our show who might not ever have been an *Oprah* viewer," said Columbia TriStar President Barry Thurston.

Meanwhile, Ancier and Steinberg examined the shows from Ricki's freshman season, determining what could be done to broaden her appeal even more. "We know how to do a relationship show very well, but we need to find a new way to do issue shows and pageant shows," Ancier said, citing a show that had the enticing title "The Search for America's Sexiest Lifeguards," which deviated from Ricki's usual mix of relationship-themed installments, but still attracted high viewer interest.

Since viewers were responding positively to Ricki, Steinberg suggested they consider the possibility of putting together shows on topics that had been considered and rejected during the first season because they didn't fit the format. "We will do the same proportion of issue shows, but I think that we may be able to take on some issues that are a little thornier and more difficult," she said. "The nicest surprise about *Ricki Lake* is not only that we reached younger viewers successfully, but older viewers as well. Audiences of all ages seem to like the freshness and originality of our show. But most of all, everyone has fallen in love with Ricki!"

The second season was launched with such attention-grabbing titles as "Summer's Over and So Are We," "I'm Not the Only One Carrying His Baby," and "I'm Not Gay Anymore."

On November 3rd the amazing happened. *Variety* reported, "Columbia TriStar's *Ricki Lake* has defeated King World's perennial talk show leader, *The Oprah Winfrey Show*, by the widest margin yet in a key adult market category." During the week of October 23rd, Ricki had attracted more eighteen-to-thirty-four-year-old viewers than Oprah. The leap was significant because it was the market advertisers coveted to sell their products to. Ricki's camp, however, remained matter-of-fact about the news. "The truth of the matter is that Oprah and Ricki are very different in many ways," Steinberg said. "No one is going to be a better

Oprah than Oprah. Hopefully, Ricki will be the best Ricki she can be."

On Thursday, December 22nd, *The Hollywood Reporter* revealed that Columbia TriStar Television was requesting double- and triple-digit increases on weekly license fees for renewals of *Ricki Lake*. Sources indicated that *Ricki*'s weekly license fee at KPHO-TV in Phoenix rose from three thousand five hundred dollars to thirty-five thousand. KPHO's station general manager, Patrick North, denied the report. He conceded that there was a significant increase, but that it wasn't anywhere near the figures that had been listed. WPWR-TV, in Chicago, paid a reported thirty-five-thousand-dollar weekly license fee for *Ricki,* which was roughly double what the station was paying the first year. KRON-TV, in San Francisco, paid a reported thirty thousand dollars, also nearly double what they were paying in the first season. KSTW-TV, in Seattle, reportedly paid eight thousand dollars, up from three thousand dollars. "It's a hit show, it's a hot item," said Dick Kurlander, vice president-director of programming at Petry Television in New York. "It's reasonable that the license fees should go up."

When the season-to-date ratings were tallied in early December, Ricki's audience had increased from one-point-nine to a high of five-point-nine, according to A.C. Nielsen Company's ratings. Out of ninety-four programs syndicated during the season, Ricki's show ranked eighteen. *Ricki Lake* was also the second highest-rated talk show behind *The Oprah Winfrey Show*.

Ricki's dramatic growth spurred other talk shows, such as *Jenny Jones, The Montel Williams Show* and *Jerry Springer* to try to emulate her success by also featuring relationship-topic shows. Like Ricki, the other programs also watched their ratings rise. But *Ricki* was clearly the leader. Besides the hefty increase in licensing fees, *Ricki*'s ratings were also up seventy-five percent in women eighteen to thirty-four, and sixty-five percent in women eighteen to forty-nine. *Ricki*'s overall household ratings had increased twenty percent, while the women-eighteen-to-thirty-four audience grew eight percent.

Of course, there was a downside to the success Ricki was enjoying. Not all the attention Ricki received was positive. *TV Guide*'s resident critic, Jeff Jarvis, panned her talk show. "I like Ricki Lake. I'm a big fan of hers," he said. "But when she started, she vowed, as they all do, that her show would be different; and like all the others, it's not. She has the same topics every one else has. Talk shows have become too often a place for people to exhibit their dirty laundry. What's tragic, in the case of *Ricki Lake*, is that it brings that pastime to a new generation. You have people screaming and crying, saying stuff like, 'No, I never loved you, but I slept with you anyway.' I fault Ricki Lake no more than the other shows, but I say, 'Oh, shucks, there goes another chance to change it.'"

In response, Gail Steinberg, who considered Jarvis's comments as "unfair" simplification, said, "When people come on [our show] to tell their stories, they try to work things out and come to a resolution. I don't consider that dirty laundry. When I was growing up in Skokie, Illinois, everyone sat on their front porches talking. Those were the talk shows of our time. It would be one thing to just have great guests tell their stories and not derive any benefit from it. That would be exploitive. We always try to have some kind of resolution by the end of our hour."

Several months after *TV Guide*'s negative review, *Time Magazine* wrote a story stating, "Ricki Lake and her disciples have achieved the impossible; lowered the standards of TV gabfests." The scorching article bemoaned the state of television talk shows in general, aiming most of its ammunition towards Ricki. A portion of the article read, "Her impact on TV has been enormous. Such competitors as Jerry Springer, Montel Williams and

Jenny Jones have gravitated toward her subject matter and her high-pitched style—and have seen their ratings jump."

Although Ricki and her producers wisely chose to stay out of the fray, and not give further fuel to the article by lending quotes, talk show host Jerry Springer defended the form. "The closer you get on live, unscripted TV to reality and its raw emotions, the rougher it's going to be. . . . Maybe our show can help people learn to tolerate differences. And maybe we can learn that everybody is capable of pain."

Meanwhile, Phil Donahue added, "I do think there's an awful lot of heavy breathing out there on the part of the so-called mainstream media. What is all the hand-wringing about? Yes, there is an entertainment feature to this. But why should the producers apologize for that? They'd better be entertaining or nobody's going to watch."

Ricki's ability to bounce back from such stinging criticism was a reflection of how much she had grown in the last two years. "Being liked used to be the end-all for me. That's what made me happy," she told a reporter. But as Ricki continued to evolve, she realized not everyone was going to appreciate or enjoy what she had to offer, either personally or professionally. Instead, she focused on accomplishing goals that brought her satisfaction.

* * *

That same season, there was also trouble brewing on Ricki's program. On her November 22nd show, Ricki featured a guest named Gwen, who was in her early thirties. Gwen revealed to the audience that she had AIDS and was HIV-positive. When Ricki asked what impact it had on Gwen's life, Gwen told the audience it was her goal to have unprotected sex with as many people as possible. Gwen added that when she died, she wanted her tombstone to read, "She took ten thousand men with her when she died." As expected, Ricki's audience was repulsed and shocked by Gwen's heartless and self-centered attitude. But Gwen merely responded, "I want people to remember me by what I did. When I get together with men I say, 'Do you want a condom?' They say, 'No,' and I smile and think, 'You're going to die.' " Gwen also revealed that she had been physically intimate with members of the vice squad in New Orleans, her hometown. "One half of the New Orleans Police Department is going to die," she said.

Two days later AP reported that "Gwendolyn Marreo, who claimed to have infected 'half the New Orleans Police Department,' did not have AIDS. She had made up the story because she wanted 'to be seen on national television.' She said the more sensational she made her story the better her chance would be of being invited back. She adds," the story said, "she's a chronic liar."

In another incident that happened at the tail end of Ricki's first season, two women contacted *Ricki Lake* and said they were quarreling roommates and that their fights were so severe they often came to blows. When Ricki's staff ran a preliminary check on the women's backgrounds, their story appeared to be accurate. But from the moment they appeared onstage, Steinberg felt a red flag go up. After watching their body language, as well as their incessant giggling, Steinberg stopped the taping. She approached the two women and said she suspected they weren't being honest. She also added that if their story was a fraud, action would be taken against them.

Soon after, Ricki's staff discovered that the women had supplied the name of a phony landlord and that their story didn't hold up. A lawyer who represented Sony Television Group, the parent company of Ricki's syndicator, sent a letter to the women demanding "immediate reimbursement of a couple of thousand dollars in airfare, ground transportation, meals, accommodations and routine per diem expenses." Steinberg said, "We're taking a very, very strong position. The biggest fear of a talk show is that you're going to be scammed."

From that point on, segment producers were directed to warn guests that when they accepted an invitation to appear on *Ricki Lake* they were in effect declaring their story to be true. Guests were then given a release to sign that stated in clear, concise language that legal action would be taken against those who lie. "No show I've worked on has enforced the kind of standards I am," said Steinberg. "It's really important to the integrity of talk television that the stories we are presenting are true stories."

Ricki was also learning that when the red light went on, she was the only one out there representing the show. Consequently, she was also the only one feeling the heat. In a show from her first season, Ricki was forced to contend with a minister from Topeka, Kansas, who crusaded against gays. He scoured newspaper obituaries for the names of men who died from AIDS and then picketed their funerals. When audience members challenged his comments, the minister merely responded, "You're going to Hell." But he saved his most vicious venom for Ricki, who was struggling to remain objective and still present a balanced show with opposing viewpoints. Angered by Ricki's unwillingness to rally to his cause, the minister blurted out, "You worship your rectum!"

Ricki was rendered speechless. "I guess he was talking to me like I was a gay man or something," she later said. "I have no idea. I didn't know what to say, I was so dumbfounded." Ricki managed to maintain her cool on the air, but during a break, she pleaded with her producers not to send her back out to contend with the minister.

Nevertheless, when the commercial was over, Ricki resumed moderating the show. It was an instance where Ricki would've preferred not being in the spotlight. "He didn't give me respect. He just didn't respect me," she said. "And it's just me out there. When we're actually doing the show, it's just me. And part of me is, like, I'm only twenty-five!"

One sure sign of Ricki's success was the new talk shows being developed to compete with her program. The names read like a "Who's Who of Young Hollywood" and included singer Carnie Wilson, Melissa Rivers (ironically, both had auditioned for Ricki's job), Danny Bonaduce (a former child star of the seventies' sitcom *The Partridge Family*), and Gabriella Carteris. *The Cosby Show*'s Tempestt Bledsoe also had a show in the works, but it was designed to be a companion piece to Ricki's program and would also be distributed by Columbia TriStar Television.

"Everyone is looking for the next good idea," said Larry Gerbrandt, vice president at Paul Kagan Associates, a research firm. Gerbrandt, however, cautioned against direct imitations of Ricki's program. "You can't just take two black females and say this will work—just because Oprah works doesn't mean Rolanda will, too," he pointed out.

Rick Jacobson, of Tribune Syndication, which launched its own Ricki-influenced show in January 1995, *The Charles Perez Show,* hosted by a former *Ricki Lake* producer, said, "Obviously, you look at the success of *Ricki Lake* and you say, 'Boy, we should be doing that.' "

The media also started closely watching Ricki's weight to see if, along with her new success, she was gaining any extra pounds. According to a report in a supermarket tabloid, Ricki was neglecting her diet and binging on pizza and gourmet foods. Sources who were supposedly close to Ricki dropped the blame at her husband Rob's feet. "Part of the problem is Rob. He loves to go out to dinner at trendy gourmet restaurants and order three or four appetizers, drinks, fattening entrees and mouth-watering desserts," said one source. A second source added, "Ricki is trying less and less to stay in shape now that she's married." Finally, a third offered, "Ricki can't resist. She loves to eat out. Like many people, she thinks that one little piece of chocolate mousse won't do any harm, but put it together with ravioli in butter sauce and that spells trouble." Meanwhile, Ricki's appearance on her daily talk show clearly demonstrated that she wasn't "putting on extra pounds."

Oprah went through a similar experience after her highly publicized weight loss in 1988. Every week, the tabloids were filled with reports that she was on eating binges. "Every time I saw something printed in the tabloids, I'd just cringe," she said. "I was in a restaurant with my staff one night. I was not eating anything and it was printed in the paper the next day that I was popping shrimps down like popcorn. What offended me was that I didn't eat anything. If I had been doing that, I would have expected that to be printed. Two days later, the waiter called the paper and said he didn't serve me anything, so I was vindicated. That's why I stopped going to my diet classes. I started out in the main sessions like everyone else, eighteen fat people sitting in a circle. But everything I said got printed in the paper." Oprah eventually learned to develop a thick skin. When she finally ran across a headline that read, "Oprah Winfrey Diet Disaster!" she didn't even bat an eye. "I remember a time I would have just been destroyed. I would have felt that I let America down—that everybody who is dieting now is going to think I'm a failure and that people are going to quit because of me. But for the first time, I looked at it, read it, and I moved on. I never thought another thing about it. For the first time. Now I know I'm growing up." Like Oprah, Ricki also learned to find herself bemused by the tabloids.

Three months after her second season began, however, Ricki found herself involved in a protest that made headlines in the mainstream newspapers, as well as the tabloids.

15

"Ricki Gets Arrested"

It was a week that started out on a good note for Ricki. Monday began with a cover story on Ricki in *People* magazine hitting the newsstands. That Tuesday she was slated to appear on *The Late Show with David Letterman*. But first Ricki got arrested.

On Monday afternoon, November 14th, Ricki, her husband Rob, and thirteen other people accompanied by camera crews, walked into designer Karl Lagerfeld's sixteenth-floor executive office at 730 Fifth Avenue at one-fifty-five P.M. and systematically began pasting anti-fur bumper stickers to the walls and furniture, yelling such slogans as "Fur is murder!" through a bullhorn. Although there wasn't fur in the offices, they also pasted bumper stickers to shoes, dresses and belts. According to the police, some members of the group rifled through a couple of desk drawers. When they were finished, the assembled group handcuffed themselves together. Meanwhile, a rankled Karl Lagerfeld executive immediately phoned the police.

Ricki was participating in an anti-fur demonstration organized by the People for Ethical Treatment of Animals (PETA). It was her first demonstration and she appeared in good spirits, chatting with Rob as she sat comfortably on the floor. "Ricki has been a longtime PETA member," said group spokeswoman Jennifer Bofinger. "This is her initiation by fire into the anti-fur cause. We can't express how happy we are she's helping us to get the issues out.

"Lagerfeld is out of touch with the young designers of today. He is a dinosaur designer who's decided to stay with fur despite the fact that the rest of the world is evolving without it."

In the past few years, such celebrities as Kim Basinger, Alec Baldwin and model Christy Turlington had also had their names associated with PETA. The protest that included Ricki was organized to take place on an afternoon when her show wasn't taping.

Within minutes after the demonstration began, the police arrived. They listened to complaints lodged by Lagerfeld executives, and then directed the group to uncuff themselves and leave the premises. According to the police, when they refused to leave, Ricki and her companions were charged with criminal mischief and third-degree burglary. "She was charged with burglary because she went into an office unlawfully," said Officer John Galway of the New York City police. Police also added that there was more than thirty-five hundred dollars in damages at the Lagerfeld executive offices. Although Karl Lagerfeld wasn't present at the time, police said his executives appeared very upset by the incident.

Ricki talked with reporters who were present and said, "I'm a freak for animals." When reporters asked how her producers felt about her participation in the protest, she responded, "They don't know about it yet. But they will! I do so much publicity for the show. This I'm doing for me. Besides, it's only a misdemeanor."

Unfortunately, Ricki had been misinformed. Since she was charged with criminal mischief and third-degree burglary, it was considered a felony— which netted far stricter penalties than a misdemeanor, including a potentially lengthy stretch in jail.

As it stood, Ricki and Rob were forced to spend a night in jail, along with the other protestors. Using a phone, Ricki made arrangements for a friend to care for her animals.

Twenty-four hours after her arrest, Ricki was released outside the back door of the Criminal Court Building. "I'm happy to be out," she told reporters. "They treated me very well." Rather than heading home, Ricki went directly to The Ed Sullivan Theater, with barely enough time to make her scheduled appearance on *The Late Show with David Letterman*.

Meanwhile, Ricki's arrest was front-page news on papers across America. It was also mentioned on several newscasts. Naturally, Letterman was anxious to talk with Ricki about her arrest. When he asked if the demonstration was part of a stunt to gain publicity for her talk show, Ricki answered, "We're the number-two show behind *Oprah*, we don't need any more ratings! Well, maybe Columbia might like more ratings." During the interview, Ricki also commented that her biggest sacrifice was missing her favorite prime-time soap, *Melrose Place*.

Letterman wasn't the only one who wondered if the stunt had been organized with the help of Ricki's producers, particularly in light of her cover story in *People*. Several columnists who blasted Ricki for participating in the protest also noted that the event took place during November sweeps, when producers work feverishly to attract as many viewers as possible because it's a period when advertising rates are set.

On the same day Ricki was released, a statement was issued by *Ricki Lake* that read:

"Ricki Lake's participation in yesterday's PETA demonstration was a personal choice driven by her belief that animals should not be killed in order to make fur coats. Her goal was to heighten the public's consciousness of this issue.

"There are rumors circulating in the media that this was a publicity stunt orchestrated by *Ricki Lake*. These rumors are categorically not true. Neither *Ricki Lake* nor any members of its staff had any involvement in the planning or execution of yesterday's PETA activities. Also, Ricki Lake's scheduled appearance this evening on *The Late Show with David Letterman* was booked more than a week ago and was arranged with no knowledge of yesterday's activities.

"As for the show, it's business as usual. The demonstration did not interrupt the production or any show activities. Per our normal taping schedule, *Ricki Lake* will tape two episodes tomorrow, Wednesday, November 16. At this time, the ethical treatment of animals is not a planned topic for the series, which will continue to focus on the popular relationship-oriented topics that have struck a chord with viewers across the country."

A few days later, Ricki's executive producer, Garth Ancier, wrote a letter to the *New York Post*, saying, "The sad fact is that Ricki was 'used' by PETA for their own purposes even beyond what was reported. She was told they would peacefully demonstrate at the Fur Department of Saks Fifth Avenue (a public place) with no destruction of property whatsoever. On the day of the protest, PETA activists changed the venue to a private office, tipped camera crews and frankly, upped the ante, without Ricki's knowledge." Acknowledging the camera crews that were present during the demonstration, Ancier added, "Video crews were called by PETA without Ricki's knowledge or approval."

"This whole thing is a classic PETA operation," said a source at NBC's *Dateline*. "I think you can assume that they bring in the biggest celebrities that they can in hopes of getting publicity for their message by whatever means necessary."

Meanwhile, Dan Matthews, PETA's director of international campaigns, who was also arrested at the demonstration that included Ricki, talked with the press, but he wouldn't confirm if there had been a late change in plans to alter the course of the protest. However, he did say, "I think PETA's relationship to its celebrity spokespeople is often frustrating to publicists because our relationship is very direct and it sometimes frustrates the spin publicists like to put on things."

Amanda Bate, a PETA spokesperson, said Ricki had been told she could be arrested for participating in the demonstration. "She chose to go ahead with the demonstration because she ardently opposes slaughtering animals to make fur coats," she added.

On December 5th, Ricki pleaded innocent in Manhattan Criminal Court to charges she helped trash the offices of fashion designer Karl Lagerfeld. She faced charges of criminal trespassing and mischief, which had been dropped to misdemeanors, but which still carried a potential maximum jail term of one year. Soon after, Ricki and Rob were each sentenced to pay a fine.

News of Ricki's arrest generated support from several surprising sources, including lawyer Raoul Felder. After making an appearance on Comedy Central's *Politically Incorrect,* he was surprised to discover his appearance earned him five hundred dollars. Raoul accepted the money and sent it directly to PETA, along with a note that read, "Please use the attached funds for Ricki Lake's legal expenses arising from her anti-fur protest at Karl Lagerfeld's offices."

Director Robert Altman, as well as Miramax pictures, also got involved in the cause to help Ricki. Altman and Miramax offered to pay the more than thirteen thousand dollars in fines expected to be levied against Ricki and the other members of PETA who were involved in the demonstration at Lagerfeld's office. Several months earlier, Altman had met Lagerfeld when he was filming *Ready to Wear,* which used the fashion world as its backdrop. Lagerfeld was the only designer who wouldn't grant Altman and his film crew access to his spring Paris show. At the time, Lagerfeld had told reporters, "Everyone who attends a show that Altman covers will remember only his film and the clothes. I'm afraid he'll make fashion look like a nightmarish cartoon." Peeved by Lagerfeld's comments, Altman relished the opportunity to have a little good-natured fun at the designer's expense by publicly lending support to Ricki and the PETA members.

Meanwhile, Ricki looked forward to closing the chapter on her fleeting experience with public demonstrations.

EPILOGUE

"Future Plans"

Imagining what her life could possibly be like in ten years, Ricki said, "If my worst-case scenario is that I'm still hosting this show in ten years, I'm going to be a very rich lady and I could retire and do whatever I want. But I have other aspirations. Now that I've met the man I am to spend the rest of my life with, I want a family, I want to have a life. And we want to work on projects together."

One of the projects Ricki wanted to work on with Rob was a children's book about an overweight girl who gets a part in a school play. "He'd do the illustrations and I would write the story. People have been after me to write the story of how I turned my weight—what many considered a handicap—into an asset. I don't know if I'm ready to do my autobiography, but a children's book about that would be good." Ricki was also excited about doing a children's book that involved an overweight child because it was a subject that had rarely been explored. "It's a great story for overweight kids. I mean, when I was little I didn't have any books to turn to other than *Blubber,* by Judy Blume. Our book would be beneficial for a lot of kids."

Plans for the book, however, were put on the back burner because Ricki's husband Rob wanted to focus on getting further along in his career before working with his wife on a project. "I'm wary of getting involved with any collaboration with Ricki before I do more on my own," he explained.

In a field as competitive as talk shows, it'd be easy for Ricki to feel territorial about "the new kids on the block," such as Carnie Wilson and Melissa Rivers, who hoped to establish themselves as voices of the younger generation with their own talk shows. Ricki, however, felt confident that her audience would remain loyal, and even wished her competitors good fortune. "I've known Carnie and Melissa for years, and now I'm helping them land jobs. I mean, when we came on the air, everyone was trying to be the new Oprah, and now everyone's trying to be the new Ricki." She also added, "I think there's more than enough audience out there that anyone can have a talk show."

Meanwhile, Ricki was looking forward to acting again during her hiatus from the show. When

Ricki was overweight, people constantly told her there was one part she was destined to play, the late singer Cass Elliott, formerly of the Mamas and Papas. "That would be the hardest thing, to portray somebody like that," she said at the time. "But I started out as a singer."

With her new trimmed-down figure, however, the field was open for Ricki to play a wider range of characters that didn't limit her to one type. To gain a higher profile in Hollywood, Ricki signed with the powerful Brillstein/Grey Entertainment management company, which represented such popular entertainers as Gary Shandling and Chevy Chase. Ricki, who was also represented by the William Morris talent agency, was already familiar with Brillstein/Grey Entertainment because they had an overall distribution deal with Columbia TriStar TV Distribution, which produced Ricki's talk show.

Although Ricki was anxious to star in movies again, she said, "I'm not going out to be Winona Ryder or something. I don't want megastardom and I don't want the level of fame of a Demi Moore. I don't want the pressure. I just want to be able to work. Now I only have thirteen weeks out of the year that I can act, but the show's good for me because the visibility is unbelievable. It makes me kind of wanted."

After her second season of *Ricki Lake* wrapped in mid-May, Ricki began work on the feature film *Mrs. Winterbourne,* a romantic comedy based on mistaken identity and formerly titled *I Married a Dead Man.* Dale Pollock, whose A&M Films produced the movie, had high hopes for the new direction Ricki's film career was taking as a romantic lead, and said, "She could emerge as a star, far different from the overweight character she played. Clearly, she's not a talk host trying to become an actress. She's a talk host who is an actress whose image was defined by her weight. Now, she has a chance to reconstitute her image by working again. For us, she's great casting."

Speaking of her role in *Mrs. Winterbourne,* Ricki said, "What I like is that the character isn't a loser who doesn't feel good about herself, which I was getting a lot of. She's a nineteen-year-old babe. This movie puts me in a whole different category altogether." She added, "Thank God, I don't ever have to play the fat girl again who can't get the nice guy. I can play a normal girl. It's a nice place to be, up against Marisa Tomei and Winona Ryder. There's more competition, but I'm ready to compete."

To prepare for her film role in *Mrs. Winterbourne,* a disciplined Ricki worked diligently to lose fifteen more pounds before filming started. To help reach her goal she opted for a more vegetarian diet. "I can't let fifteen pounds stand in my way of being a leading lady," she said.

Following *Mrs. Winterbourne*, Ricki was set to star in a film for New Line titled *Love, Gracie*, written by Aimee Pitts. Ricki's management team also met with Steven Spielberg's Amblin Production company to discuss Ricki's possible participation as lead actress in another romantic comedy, *Body Language*. There was also the possibility of more work in a New Line picture titled *The Truth about Cats and Dogs*.

As Ricki's able-bodied management team worked to line up new film roles for Ricki, she thought about her future. "I don't know what's going to happen, but I realize how lucky I am. And it feels excellent. I love the interaction with the audience. It's like I make two hundred friends every single day and for some reason the audience is on my side. That's really what is so gratifying, is that all these people are nice to me. That was my goal from childhood—not to be the smartest or the best cheerleader, but simply to be liked by everyone," she said. "Before I'm thirty, I'd like to have kids. And I want to continue acting. But for right now, doing a movie a year, the show, paying my rent and having a nice life is all I can handle."

☐	Oprah!	Robert Waldron	£5.99
☐	Cher: Her Life and Wild Times	Lawrence J Quirk	£5.99
☐	Depardieu: A Biography	Marianne Gray	£5.99
☐	Pfeiffer: Beyond the Age of Innocence	Douglas Thompson	£5.99
☐	A Time to Speak	Anthony Quayle	£6.99
☐	My Story	Ingrid Bergman	£6.99
☐	Jack Nicholson	Douglas Shepherd	£4.99
☐	Al Pacino	Andrew Yule	£5.99
☐	Jean Harlow	Irving Shulman	£5.99
☐	Bette and Joan: The Divine Feud	Shaun Considine	£5.99

Warner Books now offers an exciting range of quality titles by both established and new authors which can be ordered from the following address:

Little, Brown and Company (UK),
P.O. Box 11,
Falmouth,
Cornwall TR10 9EN.

Fax No. 01326 317444.
Telephone No: 01326 317200
E-mauil: books@barni.avel.co.uk

Payments can be made as follows: cheque, postal order (payable to Little, Brown and Company) or by credit cards, Visa/Access. Do not send cash or currency. UK customers and B.F.P.O. please allow £1.00 for postage and packing for the first book, plus 50p for the second book, plus 30p for each additional book up to a maximum charge of £3.00 (7 books plus).

Overseas customers including Ireland, please allow £2.00 for the first book plus £1.00 for the second book, plus 50p for each additional book.

NAME (Block Letters) ....

....

ADDRESS ....

....

....

☐ I enclose my remittance for ....

☐ I wish to pay by Access/Visa Card

Number ☐☐☐☐☐☐☐☐☐☐☐☐☐☐☐☐

Card Expiry Date ☐☐☐☐